Acknowledgements

Many people have put their own researches at my disposal and in particular I would like to thank Kenneth Walker, Tim Rose, Clifford Temple, Tony Harper, Jack Mitchley, Basil Craggs and Norman Jacobs. John Burrage's help with the photographs used to illustrate this book is greatly appreciated. Vallery Eke proved a far better typist than myself and Peter Allards's knowledge of Great Yarmouth was invaluable.

Numerous organisations have assisted me over the years and in particular I would like to mention The Paddle Steamer Preservation Society, The Pleasure Steamer Historical Trust, The Captain and crew of the *T. S. Orwell* at Ipswich, The *Medway Queen* Preservation Society, Yarmouth Maritime Museum, The National Maritime Museum, The Imperial War Museum, The Public Records Office at Kew, Glasgow University and the National Newspaper Library. The staffs of numerous Public Libraries, particularly Bristol, Clacton-on-Sea, Dumbarton, Glasgow, Lowestoft, Margate, Great Yarmouth, Norwich, Southampton, Portsmouth and Torquay, were of great assistance in directing me to newspapers and periodicals. The Public Record Offices in Norwich and Ipswich proved to have a wealth of information and I must thank Susan Snell at Ipswich who gave me so much assistance with photographic material.

Other individuals have not only given information but the continual encouragement needed to maintain enthusiasm when the inevitable setbacks occur. In this respect my thanks go to my publisher, David Johnson and Dean Parkin of D.A. Parkin Research Services, the late 'Wally' Upcraft, the late C.P.F. Box and W.E. Box. Special thanks must be given to Alison Paul who arrived quite unexpectedly on the scene and brought a unique photographic collection belonging to her late mother, to which she gave me free access. I am deeply indebted to Ron Lomas who diligently read through the text time and time again, and to Bernard Cox, who encouraged me from the start and was kind enough to write the foreword. Thanks also to Stuart Craik for providing the index and lastly to my wife Hilary, who for so long has put up with me talking about paddle steamers.

Peter Box
Kessingland
October 1989

Photo Credits

Peter Allard 4, 27 (bottom) 48 (bottom); C.J. Atkins 12; Bristol City Museum 83 (bottom); Basil Craggs 43 (bottom); Trustees of the Imperial War Museum 41 (bottom) 42, 43, 125; Medway Queen Preservation Society 133; Alison Paul 104 (bottom) 106; Suffolk Record Office 19(bottom) 41 (top) 28 (top) 56 (top) 128; Mrs J. Varney 69.
All other illustrations are from the author's collection.

Contents

A beautiful view of the Clacton Belle *entering the River Yare at Gorleston shortly before the Great War. The two stern lifeboats had recently been fitted to comply with new Board of Trade regulations.*

Foreword

by Bernard Cox

The traditional reminiscence of a trip on board a paddle steamer is one of an almost cloudless azure sky, rippling waters against newly-painted plates and families embarking across a wooden gangplank holding hands with well-behaved, excited children, to be greeted by a smart, uniformed Purser who would direct them across not too crowded decks to awaiting accomodation. In reality, this scene probably existed on only a handful of occasions during each Summer season. The usual scenario would comprise a grey overcast outlook, complete with a chilling northerly breeze which would entail the wearing of extra or protective clothing and a quick dash to the warmer and more salubrious surroundings of the saloons below.

Yet the paddle steamer, wherever it plied, retained an air of passive enjoyment, sometimes erupting into a more active animation as the effect of the bar, ever open when at sea, combined with a pitch or roll in open waters became too apparent.

The importance of steam navigation on the Thames, providing access to the piers of Kent, Essex and East Anglia, cannot be over-stressed. When services first commenced road and rail communications were primitive means of transport. What better, therefore, than to take advantage of the wide spacious decking, superior cushioned seating and cuisine which reached high standards and helped considerably to quicken the time in passage. The importance of the paddle steamer as a means of commuting is emphasized by the 'Bookmakers' and 'Husbands' boats mentioned in this work, the former drawing erstwhile punters to the race course at Great Yarmouth, and the latter reuniting for the weekend those who worked in the city with their more fortunate wives and children, who were able to live comfortably in rented accomodation or in selected hotels, in what today would be termed a 'yuppie' style.

And what of the constant battle for survival amongst the competing companies? Throughout the history of pleasure steamers there is evidence of intense competition for the more lucrative routes, and the vessels of the Thames were no exception. Absorptions, changes of title and financial re-arrangements occured on several occasions with two well-known ship building companies, William Denny & Brothers of Dumbarton, and the Fairfield Shipbuilding and Engineering Company of Glasgow, taking more than a passing financial interest, no doubt influenced by the hope of further orders and subsequent profits.

Nor must we forget the wartime service of the paddle steamers in both World conflicts. Like any other class of merchant ship impressed for service, there were losses, but perhaps their remarkable achievement was their ability to thresh their way as far as the Mediterranean and even to the White Sea in the course of their wartime duties.

Perhaps the Thames-based vessels' finest hour came in May 1940 when, as we shall read, these grey-painted veterans rescued many thousands of the beleaguered British Expeditionary force, the *Medway Queen* setting up a paddle minesweeper record of no less than seven round trips to the beaches.

And what of the crews that manned excursion steamers around our coasts? For the main part they were emplyed on a seasonal basis, no job security in the Merchant Navy! Many of them would have been elderly or retired seafarers or perhaps those who, for one reason or another, did not wish to return to deep sea employment. Many of the ships' officers were also signed on in a temporary capacity, only the captain and Engineering Officers holding some power over the Company for permanent employment, their expertise being needed for the annual re-fit to which all passenger vessels were subjected, prior to the granting of a Board of Trade Certificate to sail within defined limits with a specified number of fare paying passengers.

Their hours were long, as the crew would muster some time before the first sailing of the day; nor was it a matter of a straight sailing from point A to point B, because owners, ever-conscious of profit and the fact that it had to be made within the confined of the Summer season, would not plan to let any vessel lie idle, swinging on her ropes at a pier or harbour. Even if the vessel's stay was limited to a comparatively short period, the ship would be employed on a 'trip around the bay' or short cruise to view some local well-known beauty spot. The excursions to the furthest points in the Company's routes would also involve several hours' steaming in either direction and a working day, by the time the vessel had returned to its night-time berth, would sometimes exceed fifteen hours, with the prospect of a further day's steaming on the morrow. After snatching a few hours rest on board, the crew would be busy in preparation for the next sailing. These were certainly conditions which would not be tolerated or asked for today.

Many times I have asked, "What was the main attraction of the paddle steamers?" The answer, as in all social research, can only be expressed as being the culmination of several factors. Certainly there was the thrill of travel at what today would seem a leisurely pace, but in the hey-day of the pleasure steamer would be comparable to our inter-city links. Whilst travel for some would be wholly a pleasurable experience, for others it would be a form of 'in season' commuting. Some, perhaps, saw the pleasure steamer as a means of emulating, albeit on a minor scale, their more fortunate friends or relatives who were able to participate in big ship cruising. Whilst the liner's passengers were able to view and land in countries which hitherto had only been seen on an atlas, the paddle steamer passengers during their cruise would view and land at another seaside resort of which they had heard mention by word of mouth or perhaps during some geography lesson on the British Isles. Some there were who took a marine excursion for the sake of their health, the Victorians in particular being of the opinion that invigorating sea breezes and ozone would result in the dissipation of their bronchial ailments brought about by their working days being spent in the confines of a factory or in the crowded city accomodation, where they spent their everyday lives.

But above all it must have been the sense of freedom and space provided on uncluttered decks that motivated the passenger to sail on board the Belle steamer of his choice, the history of which is unveiled in the following pages.

Introduction

One bright morning in March 1951, a tug moved slowly through the still waters of the Thames estuary. She had in tow a dilapidated paddle steamer that she was taking up-river to the ship-breakers Thomas Ward at Grays, Essex. Through the morning mist and the steamer's faded, flaking paintwork could just be seen her name; *Pride of Devon*. Now she was nobody's 'pride', just one of the hundreds of vessels that found their way to the scrap-yards of post war Britain. But, for those who witnessed her passing and knew her story, it was a sad home-coming for a vessel that had brought happiness to countless thousands for over fifty years. Most of those years had been spent on the Thames when, as *Walton Belle*, she had been one of the most popular pleasure steamers on the river and in holiday resorts from Ramsgate to Great Yarmouth. It did not take the experienced ship-breakers long to reduce this once fine steamer to a pile of unrecognisable scrap. Soon, nothing remained of the last 'Belle Steamer'.

This book is about paddle steamers and in particular that fleet known along the East Coast as the *Belle* Steamers. It traces their development from their inception at the height of the Victorian age through to their virtual extinction in the depression of the 1930s. It is both a story of a company that helped fashion many of the holiday resorts along the east coast and a story of rivalry; for without rivalry there would probably be no story. It tells of an era past, an era destined never to return. Today, all that is left are piers battling for survival against current economic demands and the forces of nature. Some, such as those at Lowestoft and Southwold, have almost lost the struggle, while others gaze towards an uncertain horizon.

Standing recently on the windswept remains of the Claremont Pier, I realised that I had been lucky to have experienced paddle steamer travel in its final years along the South Coast. Then, as a boy, I had marvelled at the smell and sounds of the old *Princess Elizabeth* as she left Swanage Pier for Bournemouth, gulls at her stern, porpoises darting below her bow and always the wind in my hair. *Embassy*, *Monarch* and *Consul* were names on the tip of my tongue and now, long gone, are memories indelibly etched in my mind. They are memories I shall always treasure and are the inspiration behind this book.

Finally, this is not a book written for the nautical specialist but for anyone who enjoys history and, like myself, has the sea in their blood.

Peter Bruff in middle age.

The Formative Years 1

In April 1865 the press announced the sale of land in the parish of Great Clacton, Essex. This 'parcel' of land, about one mile away from the village of Great Clacton, was an almost deserted spot, known locally as Clacton Beach. Until 1864 the land had been held in trust by the Watson family and development had been very limited. The track that led along the cliff was known as Rosemary Lane from the plants that grew there, and was used only by the resident farmers and the few locals for walks. The tiny hamlet of Clacton Beach was made up of coastguard and farm cottages. One of the Watson family had converted a house into a comfortable summer residence, whilst another house offered "refreshments" to locals and travellers alike! A visitor at the time commented that the "country around looked bare and bleak as far as the eye could reach".The Watson trust, while protecting the traditional way of life, had inhibited any real development and, if death had not intervened and forced a sale, then the solitary Martello tower would have remained the sole object of interest and Clacton Beach would have remained a tiny hamlet with a past, but no future.

On the demise of the trust there was opportunity for development and one Peter Schuyler Bruff of Handford Lodge, Ipswich saw the land as having great potential and purchased fifty acres. He had noticed that the estate was as far from London as was the already fashionable resort of Margate. Towns along the Kent coast had developed considerably with the growing trend towards 'taking a holiday' and Bruff saw no reason why the Essex coast should not become just as popular. Bruff himself was a notable civil engineer who, at that time, was working for the Eastern Union Railway on the construction of the line from Colchester to Walton-on-the-Naze. By 1867 this branch line had been completed but, at its nearest point, it was still some five miles from Bruff's land at Clacton Beach — the railway to Clacton was not completed until 1882 — which left a serious communication problem. The roads from the railhead to his newly-purchased estate were utterly deplorable. The rutted tracks were uncomfortable to travel along and after heavy rain became impassable. What had been acceptable to the farmer would not be to the potential backers of Bruff's enterprise or its clientele, the largely untapped and growing holiday market to be found in London. It was a developer's nightmare but, if Bruff was to develop his land, he had to solve the transport problem.

Being a man of foresight and determination he secured by Act of Parliament the necessary authorisation to allow him to build both a branch railway and a pier. Obviously, he himself lacked the capital for a scheme of such magnitude but he did have influential connections and so he set about attracting investors.

Perhaps the risk was too great and the returns too speculative, because Bruff was not altogether successful in this venture. So, in 1870, with the powers of his Act fast running out, he invited, almost it seems in desperation, a Mr. W. P. Jackson to Clacton. Jackson, an eminent and well-respected London businessman, was at the time chairman of the expanding Woolwich Steam Packet Company. This company's large fleet of paddle steamers was well known on the Thames and indeed, as far as Ipswich. For a number of years a regular packet service had been run from London to the river Orwell using the paddle steamers *Queen of the Orwell* and *Queen of the Thames*. Bruff realised that their route took them right past Clacton and that they could easily become the cornerstone of his enterprise. His task was to persuade Jackson to invest and make Clacton a port of call. We are told that the two men 'paced up and down' the windswept beach for there was nowhere else to go! After a lengthy discussion, Bruff got Jackson's backing and a start was soon made on the construction of a pier. That one meeting had solved the question of transport, and today the directors of the Woolwich Steam Packet Company are remembered in Clacton by the roads named in their honour; William Agate, James Ellis, Thomas Hayes, Abel Penfold and William Jackson.

In 1871, the year which saw the establishment of Bank Holidays, the first Clacton pier was opened amid some hostility from the local residents. With a length of only half today's structure and with no buildings, it was little more than a large jetty. However, it was all that Bruff needed to make his venture work. The first ship to call on 18 July 1871 was the *Queen of the Orwell* on her regular run to Ipswich. The more elaborate 'official' opening came nine days later on July 27th, when the larger paddle steamer *Albert Edward* made a special visit with a number of influential dignitaries aboard. The guests were met by Bruff on landing, and soon about 200 people had found their way onto the beach and the surrounding cliffs. It was from amongst this company that Bruff succeeded in finding more investors prepared to put money into his speculative venture. Perhaps he was lucky in that his guests soon had to return to the ship for the journey back to London and so had no time to become bored! The reason for their swift departure was that the short pier allowed vessels to berth only at high water!

The directors of the Woolwich Steam Packet Company were apparently well satisfied with the developments at Clacton and further investment took place. By the end of 1871 two substantial villas had been built in Rosemary Lane and these now form part of the Osborne Hotel in the centre of the town.

In the years up to 1877 the paddle steamers regularly called at the new resort but, as they were often unable to land at the pier because of the tide, they disgorged their passengers into a variety of little boats that plied to and fro from the beach. As Clacton slowly spread inland and along the beach, Bruff made sure that roads were carefully planned and that a high standard of public health and amenities was attained.

In 1877, the now totally inadequate pier was extended to its present length and buildings arose at the entrance and the pier head. This extension enabled ships to berth at all states of the tide, and although it might have proved unpopular with the beach boat owners, it was welcomed by the growing number of passengers who were flocking to the resort. A toll of two pence was levied on those wishing to promenade along its length and take in the sea air. This was a popular Victorian activity, as the large number of very ornate South Coast piers of this period testify, but it is important to realise that Bruff's pier was primarily a place of work, where cargoes were landed and loaded. Costs varied from a penny for each cubic foot of musical instrument to one pound if you were unfortunate enough to require the landing of a corpse! By this date the Woolwich Steam Packet Company had merged with other shipping concerns to become the London Steamboat Company and were sending at least two ships to Clacton each day.

By 1880 muddy Rosemary Lane had become fashionable Pier Avenue and Rosemary Road. Fine hotels and boarding houses graced the thoroughfares of this now fashionable resort. Before his death in 1900, Bruff witnessed the meteoric rise of Clacton as a resort and also the development of a shipping company that would become the 'Belle Steamers'.

Although *Belle Steamers* had yet to be conceived, the development of Clacton was fundamental to their conception. The second, no less important thread in their story, is provided by the growth in passenger services along the river Thames.

The Woolwich Steam Packet Company was just one of a number of steamboat companies that had developed on the river. It had been formed as early as 1834 and each day ran local services between Charing Cross and Woolwich. Although at the time their paddle steamers were regarded as being the most uncomfortable vessels on the river, the nature of their services made them very popular. The Company had taken advantage of the advances made in paddle steamer construction and the fact that the railway companies had yet to develop a transport network along either bank of the Thames. Quite simply, the paddle steamers were the quickest and most effective form of transport along the river. The company grew, absorbing smaller shipping concerns and extending its routes down river to Southend and the Kent ports. By 1871 the Woolwich Steam Packet Company had come to monopolise Thames passenger traffic from Kew to Sheerness, and so it was not surprising that Bruff chose to approach this Company.

In 1876, a major amalgamation of Thames steamboat companies including the Woolwich Steam Packet Company, resulted in the formation of the London Steamboat Company. The Clacton interest was maintained by a Mr. W. Towse, who was appointed as the Traffic Superintendent. The new Company's assets now included over seventy vessels and, although many of these were up-river steamers, six of the larger, more modern vessels, were used on the established packet service to Ipswich. These ships are recorded as being the paddle steamers *Queen of the Orwell*, *Queen of the Thames*, *Duke of Connaught*, *Duke of Cambridge*, *Duke of Teck* and *Duke of Edinburgh*. Seven other vessels were used on routes to Gravesend, Southend and Sheerness and these included the Company's largest and most prestigious paddle steamers, *Alexandra*, *Princess Alice* and *Albert Edward*.

Two prominent companies were left out of this amalgamation. Firstly, there was the General Steam Navigation Company which had formed in 1824 and which, by 1870, had services that extended worldwide. They owned six Thames paddle steamers including the ''splendid saloon steamer *Hoboken*'' that had been launched in 1873. Secondly, there was the Medway Steam Packet Company which owned three steamers and operated services between the towns of Rochester, Sheerness and Southend. The successors to this Company were to play an important part in the closing chapters of our story.

The London Steamboat Company flourished under its hard-working head, John Mann, until 1878 when disaster struck the paddle steamer *Princess Alice*. This accident was a colossal blow from which it is said the London Steamboat Company never fully recovered. Accidents had happened to Thames steamers before. In August 1859 the paddle steamer *Bride* hit a submerged barge near London Bridge but, fortunately, all her passengers were taken off before she sank! Then, in March 1863, the paddle steamer *Sibyl* also struck an object at London Bridge and sank. As there had been no loss of life, the public at large seemed to accept these comparitively rare happenings and enjoyed to the full the advantages of river transport. However, the tragedy that befell the *Princess Alice* stunned not only river users, but the whole nation.

The *Princess Alice* and her sistership *Albert Edward* had long been favourites with the London public. They had been built in 1865 as *Bute* and *Kyles* respectively, for service on the Clyde. They had been purchased by the Waterman's Company in 1867 and were renamed after Queen Victoria's second daughter and her eldest son, the Prince of Wales. Both vessels were licensed to carry 936 passengers between London and Gravesend and 486 passengers, in the more open waters, to Sheerness. After the 1876 amalgamation, ownership had passed to The London Steamboat Company who used them for longer services and for excursion work during the summer season.

On 3rd September 1878, *Princess Alice* left Sheerness at 4.15 p.m. The weather was good and it promised to be a routine return trip to London Bridge. At Gravesend her complement of passengers was swollen to near capacity by 'trippists' returning home to the city. By 8.00 p.m. she was approaching Woolwich; the sun was low, the evening was drawing in and the vessel was battling against a strong ebb tide and so was hugging the south bank where the force was less. Her next port of call was to be North Woolwich Pier on the North bank and so after leaving a point known as Tripcock Trees, she headed across the tide towards the Beckton Gas Works. She was about halfway across when she encountered the collier *Bywell Castle* (1,326 gr. tons) coming down river. There was said to have arisen a misunderstanding about navigation lights but, whatever was the truth, the result was tragic. The collier ripped into the *Princess Alice* near to the starboard paddle box almost cutting her into two. The aft part of the ship sank immediately causing the bow to rise up into the air before breaking off and sinking a little further downstream. The incident was over in less than five minutes but in that short space of time almost 700 lives were lost. Whole families were drowned as bystanders stood helplessly a few hundred yards away on the shore. Among those lost were Mrs Towse and her four children. The exact number of casualties will never be known as all records were lost with the ship and there was also a widespread practice of allowing two children to travel on one adult ticket. The subsequent Board of Trade enquiry stated that the *Princess Alice* was entirely to blame for the error in navigation and censured the late Captain Grinstead for the loss of his vessel. This outcome shook the public confidence in river transport and the financial implications resulting from it were indirectly to affect the entrepreneurs of Clacton.

The London Steamboat Company's decline must also be seen in the context of London's transport systems as a whole. The *Princess Alice* disaster came at a most inopportune time, a time when land transportation along the Thames had begun

The stern of the Princess Alice *after it had been raised from the river bed. The saloons were so crowded that people were unable to escape and drowned 'standing up'. Some were later found in this macabre posture within the vessel.*

Thames Steamboat Collision Relief Fund.

No. **10**   Town Hall, Brighton, *14th octor.* 1878.

Received of *Y Reeves Smith Esq*

the sum of *One* pounds *eight* shillings and *five* pence,

being Subscription to the above Fund. — *the amount deposited*

in a collection box at the Brighton

Aquarium

£ *1 : 8 : 5*   *Fredk Dunkley*

For the Honorary Secretary.

The disaster to the Princess Alice *so shook the nation that the Mansion House set up a disaster fund. This receipt was issued to the Brighton Aquarium in respect of £1-8-5d raised by them in a collection box.*

to present a growing threat to the river boats. The penny fares charged by steamers were acceptable only as long as the omnibuses charged three pence for an equivalent journey. But, increasing competition between the omnibus companies had reduced fares within the city considerably and, as their popularity grew, it was even suggested in the press that the London public would soon forget about paddle steamers for shorter journeys. It is also interesting to note that at this date the steamboat operators paid the Thames Conservancy £6,000 for the use of its piers. They therefore needed to take one and a half million penny fares to recoup these charges alone! To make matters worse, the railway network was growing all the time and the construction of the Inner Circle and District lines was by then well advanced.

There was also increasing concern over the health risks involved in river transport, as the pollution to be found in the river was appalling. Raw sewage from the city poured into the river at a rate of about ten million cubic feet each day and articles about this problem feature prominently in newspapers of the time. The major sewage outfall was situated just below Blackwall and although schemes for its improvement had been proposed they had yet to be acted upon. In summer, the smell could be overpowering! A contemporary writer, while complaining about the colour of the Thames, recounts that the river users also had to contend with the macabre problem of "dead bodies". In one incident a "badly decomposed corpse" became entangled with the paddle wheel of an unspecified vessel, much to the disgust of those aboard. It transpired that the body had been seen floating with the tide for several days and had not been recovered because the watermen's retrieval fee had recently been stopped! Certainly the river was not the ideal place for a relaxing afternoon trip. But, nevertheless, in spite of the river's reputation and the disaster to the *Princess Alice*, the London Steamboat Company continued to trade.

In 1883 they purchased two further paddle steamers from a small rival concern, The Thames and Channel Steamship Company. As so often happened with Thames steamship companies, I suspect there was a link between The London Steamboat Company and The Channel Steamship Company as they shared the same address and some of the former's vessels appear on the latter's handbills. These vessels were the older, wooden, *Vale of Clwyd* and the more modern, iron, *Glen Rosa*. With the declining fortunes of their up-river services, the Company was seeking both to improve the quality of their fleet and their area of operations. They wished to expand, and develop services to Europe in direct competition with those of the General Steam Navigation Company which had a long established service to the French and Belgian ports. *Vale of Clwyd* had been built in 1865 for the Dunoon and Ayr summer service, while *Glen Rosa* had been built at Greenock in 1877 for a service to Arran. *Glen Rosa* was to have a nomadic existence covering forty-four years and was to feature prominently in the story of east coast paddle steamers before the turn of the century. Soon after entering service on the Clyde, *Glen Rosa's* owners had succumbed to the intense competition prevailing in that area. *Glen Rosa* came south in 1881 and was immediately put into a varied routine of service and charter work. She was comfortable and fast, being said to make twenty-one knots with a favourable tide, but I suspect that the tide would have to be very favourable for her to reach that speed. She appeared regularly along the Thames coast and in July 1881 was chartered to carry dignitaries at the opening of the new lock at Ipswich. These included the

THE "SILENT HIGHWAY"-MAN.
"Your MONEY or your LIFE!"

A cartoon published in London during the 1860s reflects the concern felt about the shocking pollution then found in the Thames.

Glen Rosa *in the colours of the London Steamboat Company, is pictured at the opening of the New Lock at Ipswich in July 1881. Peter Bruff was amongst the Ipswich dignitaries aboard at the time.*

President of the Board of Trade, the Right Hon. Joseph Chamberlain, and the Mayor of Ipswich, Alderman Wrinch.

Bruff, who was also aboard that day, must have been pleased to see such a vessel visiting Clacton. *Glen Rosa* also ran along the Kent coast to Dover and across the channel to the French ports of Dunkirk, Boulogne and Calais. Her one major failing was un-reliability and she became notorious for breakdowns and mechanical problems. We are told that the comment ''*Glen Rosa* late again'' was frequently heard at the piers.

So it was that the *Glen Rosa* and her consort *Vale of Clwyd* passed into the ownership of the ailing London Steamboat Company in 1883. In December 1884, financial pressures resulted in the Company being offered for sale in lots. The major assets were acquired by a new Company called The River Thames Steamboat Company and in this financial upheaval, Clacton lost its local interest in the shipping concern.

In 1885 the General Steam Navigation Company became aware that their small, but useful, Thames operations had become very vulnerable to competition. Indeed, they had already experienced it on their Kent, Essex and French services from both *Glen Rosa* and *Vale of Clwyd*. As a company, they were fortunate in being financially secure. Any financial problems encountered on the Thames could easily be absorbed in the profits made by their overseas trading concerns. In this respect they were quite unlike the River Thames Steamboat Company which, as their predecessors had been, were soon financially crippled by ageing steamers and unprofitable up-river routes. The General Steam Navigation Company were also far-sighted and realised that, given the right conditions, many of the longer routes down the Thames could become very profitable. What was needed was modern ships which would increase public confidence and demand, for Clacton was not the only town along the East Coast that was developing a tourist industry. With London's increasing population and the growing popularity of holidays, the opportunities for expanding the routes between Dover and Great Yarmouth were vast, and if the General Steam Navigation Company did not develop them, somebody else surely would!

In June 1886 the River Thames Steamboat Company was offered for sale. However, it seems to have found no purchaser, for in 1887 it was still operating a greatly reduced service with only six vessels available. An injection of £67,000 into the company had done nothing to alleviate the situation. During this period of contraction the company had significantly reduced their long-distance services and one of these was to Clacton. Indeed, the Clacton Pier Company had itself to arrange for it own services!

The Arrival of the Belle Steamers 2

The summer of 1887 marked the start of a period of unprecedented growth in the story of east coast paddle steamers and as such it deserves detailed consideration. It was a period of development which was to last into the next century; a period that would alter the appearance of many seaside resorts.

The General Steam Navigation Company set about consolidating their Thames operations against possible competition. They intended to extend their routes and improve their existing summer services to Kent and Great Yarmouth. To do this they took delivery of the first of five new paddle steamers, the first that the company had ordered to be constructed since the *Hoboken* some fourteen years earlier. The new General Steam Navigation vessel was named *Halcyon*, (the Greek name for the Kingfisher, a bird which according to their fable was supposed to calm the seas), an attribute that I am sure many passengers came to wish was not just a fable! She had been built by the established ship-building company of Messrs J. Scott at Kinghorn on the north bank of the Firth of Forth and at 209 feet in length and displacing 458 gross tons she was, for the Thames at that time, a sleek, luxurious steamer. Her 'modern' compound twin cylinder, two-crank diagonal engines made her capable of speeds up to 17 knots in the open waters of the Thames Estuary. On July 9th 1887 *Halcyon* ran the first of her builder's trials on the Forth. As soon as these had finished she came south and in late July, entered service on the Thames. She was just the kind of vessel required by the company to modernise its services.

J. Scott & Co. went on to build the remaining four paddle steamers ordered by The General Steam Navigation Company. Colloquially called the 'Classical Birds', these five ships were all near sisters to each other. The final four were delivered in the years up to 1889 and were named: *Mavis*, the song thrush (1888); *Oriole*, the beautiful gold and black starling (1888); *Laverock*, the lark (1889); and finally, the largest vessel, *Philomel*, the nightingale (1889). At first glance these five ships looked remarkably similar. Each had one dignified black funnel and two pole masts that gave a well-balanced profile. All the vessels had well-equipped saloons on which was placed a full width promenade deck that proved very popular with passengers when the weather permitted! The more obvious differences lay in the paddle box designs, the shape of the individual funnels and the positions of the lifeboats. Quite why these 'Classical Birds' were not identical is a mystery, since it would have certainly reduced design and building costs if they had been.

As in previous years, the 1887 General Steam Navigation service to Great Yarmouth began early in June using one of their 'continental steamers'. A number of paddle steamers were categorised as such, among which were the *Moselle*, *Seine*, *Rhine*, *Swift* and *Swallow*. As the title 'continental' implies, they were often employed on services to France and Belgium but, at other times, and especially during busy summer periods, they were used on a variety of other routes running passengers or general cargo. The *Seine*, which inaugurated the 1887 service, had been a regular visitor to Great Yarmouth in previous years and was an old vessel, having been in General Steam Navigation service for 38 years.

Although the arrival of the London steamers was important to the town, a far more significant event occurred on July 23rd. On that busy Saturday in 1887 two General Steam Navigation paddle steamers came up the Yare. The first to moor at 6.30 p.m. was the *Hoboken*, after what was described as "an unusually quick passage". It was the first time that this vessel or indeed any other deck-saloon paddle steamer had entered the port and she caused much curiosity amongst those who witnessed her arrival. Just why she caused this interest is clear when one examines her design. Today it could be likened only to Concorde arriving at your local airport! *Hoboken* had been built by Napier & Sons at Glasgow and had entered General Steam Navigation service in 1873 as the Company's first deck-saloon steamer. Comfortable saloon cabins fore and aft of the paddle boxes were connected so as to allow passengers a continuous raised promenade deck on which they could sit or stroll. Future paddle steamer designs including the 'Classical Birds' and 'Belles' would all follow this pattern. Great Yarmouth had not seen a vessel of her type before and as such her arrival marked a turning point in the story of East Coast passenger services. The second steamer to arrive that Saturday was the *Seine*, she came up the river at her usual time to berth with *Hoboken* at Hall Quay.

During August 1887 *Hoboken* was regularly employed along the East Coast running without incident. She was described in the press as being a "handsome vessel, most comfortably arranged" and she quickly established a routine. After arriving at Great Yarmouth at about 6.30 p.m. she lay overnight at Hall Quay, by Haven Bridge, and left the following morning for London Bridge (Fresh Wharf) at 8.00 a.m. unless previously full. On the 1887 August Bank Holiday Saturday she left seventy-five minutes early! At other times and particularly on busy weekends she was supplemented by up to two other vessels. General Steam Navigation were not consistent in their advertising — with a monopoly they probably had no need to be. However, potential passengers could obtain full details of the Company's services from London or from their Yarmouth agent, Mr. Stacey Watson, at Quay House. Readers may be curious about the origins of the name *Hoboken* for a Thames coast paddle steamer. *Hoboken* was probably named after a shipbuilding town in Belgium and simply reflects the Company's worldwide shipping interests.

Hoboken's arrival on the London to Great Yarmouth service coincides almost to the day with *Halcyon* entering service. Prior to 1887, *Hoboken* had been used on the prestigious and financially lucrative Kent service. So it was to these resorts that the General Steam Navigation Company sent their newest vessel, *Halcyon*. She was advertised as running to Margate, Ramsgate and the Continent. This released the older *Hoboken* for the long East Coast service.

An unusual postcard showing General Steam Navigation's old paddle steamer Swift *at Great Yarmouth. This vessel was a common visitor to the port in the years up to 1900.*

Halcyon, *easily identified by her enclosed foresaloon, is pictured at Great Yarmouth just before the turn of the century. Like all the 'Classical Birds',* Halcyon *carried a beautifully embellished badge at her bow; hers depicted a kingfisher.*

These improvements at Great Yarmouth did not help the developers of Clacton who were carefully planning the future expansion of the town, since the service provided by *Hoboken* was direct. No calls were made after leaving the Thames. To complicate matters further, during the summer the Clacton Pier Company had been engaged in a financial battle with the unreliable River Thames Steamboat Company over the pier dues. The Steamboat Company had left many bills outstanding because of their poor financial situation and the battle culminated in the Pier Company imposing a ban on River Thames Steamboat Company vessels. This was an extremely serious course of action as it has been estimated that some 25,000 passengers landed there each season, the majority from River Thames Steamboat Company vessels. Quite naturally, concern was voiced in the town as passenger traffic was vital to Clacton's prosperity. Thus, through exasperation as much as from necessity, a group of businessmen together with the Pier Company decided to form a steamship company of their own. It is interesting to note that the principal shareholders were those of the earlier Woolwich Steam Packet Company. The only Clacton subscriber was Mr. Wallis, proprietor of the Royal Hotel. Abel Penfold was appointed chairman and Horace Spence as its general manager. Offices were acquired at 33, Walbrook in the City of London. These offices were not far from the river and the established steamer boarding points at Fresh Wharf and Old Swan Pier. The new Company was registered on July 23rd 1887 under the name of the London, Woolwich and Clacton-on-Sea Steamboat Company, a title that reflected the areas in which financial backing had been found. The directors decided to have built a paddle steamer of their own; a ship designed and operated to meet their specific needs. So, the competition anticipated by The General Steam Navigation Company had materialised.

Such a venture was a financial risk but one deemed to be worth taking even though another small shipping venture involving Clacton had failed in that September. It was a decision perfectly in keeping with the town's entrepreneurial spirit. The failure had involved a paddle steamer named *Bonnie Doon*, which had been built by T. B. Sneath of Glasgow in 1876 for use on the Clyde. On the demise of her service between Glasgow and Ayr she had embarked on a varied career of charter work that led her to the Thames in August 1887. On Saturdays, Sundays and Mondays *Bonnie Doon* sailed from Fresh Wharf just below London Bridge, to Clacton via Greenwich, Blackwall and North Woolwich, returning the same day. On Tuesdays, Wednesdays and Fridays she went to the busy port of Sheerness via Southend, Gravesend and, nearby, the fashionable Pleasure Gardens at Rosherville.

Rosherville had been founded by Jeremiah Rosher in 1859 on the site of an old quarry. It was described at the time as a place in which ''to spend a happy day'' and was not surprisingly, a regular stop for Thames steamers. *Bonnie Doon*'s Thursday itinerary was different in that it included an excursion ''round the Girdler'', a light-vessel well out in the Thames Estuary. After the trouble caused by the gradual demise of the River Thames Steamboat Company the ship must have been welcomed by the Clacton community and, perhaps, even more so when in late August *Bonnie Doon*'s service was changed to make Clacton a daily port of call. However, it appears that for some reason these operations were not a success and some dissatisfaction was expressed in Clacton. All advertisements for *Bonnie Doon* ceased after September 15th. This was a date not far from the normal end to the summer season, but nevertheless it transpired that the end was premature. Debts had mounted and the vessel's charterer, Richard Ford, was taken to Court. The sums of money involved give some indication as to what was paid to the crews of paddle steamers. Her Captain, Samuel Mason (at one time the captain of *Glen Rosa*) was paid seven pounds a week and was owed for three! The chief steward Joseph Haw earned two pounds a week and he appears not to have received the ten pound gratuity promised on the cessation of the service. Also, a wage of one pound sixteen shillings was supposed to have been paid to Samuel Middleton for "swinging and mooring" the vessel in London. The Court case further revealed that *Bonnie Doon* had stopped operating because her coal bill was unpaid and the merchants would not supply any more. The magistrate ordered the amounts to be paid and subsequently *Bonnie Doon* returned to her previous base at Bristol where, after numerous other charters, she passed into the ownership of the much respected paddle steamer operators, P. & A. Campbell. She provided services for them along the south coast and Bristol Channel before being towed to Rotterdam in November 1913 where she was scrapped.

A point of interest worth mentioning here is that it was deemed quite acceptable for Thames paddle steamers to operate on Sundays, but this was not the case in all areas. On the south coast and in Scotland 'sabbath breaking' evoked bitter controversy and was not permitted for many years. On the east coast some problems were later experienced when pier entertainments contravened local bylaws but these were, in the main, quickly overcome.

The London, Woolwich and Clacton-on-Sea Steamboat Company ignored the sceptics and chose instead to learn from the mistakes of others. Accordingly, they placed an order for a paddle steamer with the shipyard of Messrs J. Scott at Kinghorn. Presumably they had been impressed both by the workmanship in *Halcyon* and the speed of delivery. Their new vessel, appropriately named *Clacton*, was launched on May 8th 1888. Built of steel, she was 189.5 feet in length and displaced 241 gross tons. Her spacious saloon extended over the full width of the vessel and at the stern opened out onto a small covered quarterdeck on which passengers could relax in comfort. Beneath was a well-equipped dining saloon that would meet the needs of excursionist and businessman alike. A small steamer, *Clacton* reached a speed of sixteen knots on trials and although this was not fast, it was thought to be quite adequate by her future owners who were on board at the time. The London, Woolwich and Clacton-on-Sea Steamboat Company decided to use Old Swan Pier as their London boarding point and as this was just up-river from London Bridge it had some important design implications. To enable the ship to pass between the arches of the bridge *Clacton* was equipped with a hinged foremast and telescopic funnel. Strangely, the rake of the mast did not match that of the funnel and this tended to spoil the look of the vessel.

Clacton entered service on May 17th 1888. She left London daily at 9.30 a.m., except for Fridays, which was regarded as a 'make and mend' day, and proceeded to Clacton where she arrived at about 2.30 p.m. Later she would return to London arriving alongside Old Swan Pier at about 8.30 p.m.

In addition to the *Clacton*, the Thames services for 1888 were further enriched by the appearance of the next two 'Classical Birds' of the General Steam Navigation Company, *Mavis* and *Oriole*. While the new vessels remained on the Thames, the *Hoboken* was again regularly employed on the direct service to Great Yarmouth, running on Wednesdays and Saturdays only. On Yarmouth race-days she ran a special service which was well patronised by the London racing fraternity and this was often referred to as the "book-maker's boat". The number of passengers using the Great Yarmouth service was gradually increasing in spite of the competition from other "aristocratic seaside resorts" and the direct railway link via Norwich. *Hoboken* regularly carried a complement of 500 persons, always referred to in the press as "freight" and on the August Bank Holiday Saturday she was supported by three other vessels. By the end of August the new *Mavis* was regularly supporting *Hoboken* and *Seine* on the service. Reports suggest that the numbers disembarking from vessels were about double those of 1886, and this was in spite of weather that was recognised as being the worst experienced for many years. The potential passenger trade with Great Yarmouth was great and was increasing all the time.

In February 1888 the serviceable vessels in the River Thames Steamboat Company fleet were taken over by an association of business interests developed solely for this purpose. A new Company was formed under the regal title of the Victoria Steamboat Association. Their offices were in Cannon Street, London, close to the river piers and its General Manager was one Edgar Shand. He had previously been manager of the Thames and Channel Steamship Company which, as was mentioned earlier, had close links with the London Steamboat Company. The ambitious Victoria Steamboat Association scrapped unwanted vessels and looked about for others that would rival the 'Classical Birds'. They desperately needed to update their services if they were to rival the now dominant General Steam Navigation Company.

Their services for the summer of 1888 were quite extensive ranging from the Thames to Ipswich, Dover and across to France. At Ipswich *Glen Rosa*, sporting a new telescopic funnel, was a regular visitor under the command of Captain Edward Mills. There, dubiously described as "one of the fastest steamers in the world", she ran a three times weekly service to Old Swan Pier, stopping at Ha'penny Pier Harwich, Walton-on-the-Naze and Clacton. From there she crossed to Gravesend and Rosherville before proceeding up-river to North Woolwich, Blackwall and Greenwich. On alternate days the *Glen Rosa* found herself running down the Thames to Clacton in direct competition with the *Clacton*. The two companies soon began to argue about sailing times and routes and, by September the squabbling had spread to the paddle steamer crews. Eventually an Inspector of the Victoria Steamboat Association struck the caterer of the *Clacton* on Old Swan Pier and immediately a *fracas* began. One can only speculate as to what passengers thought of such behaviour! On Sundays during July, *Glen Rosa* ran sea excursions. A popular trip was from Ipswich to Margate where passengers were guaranteed one hour ashore but the cost, four shillings and sixpence return, would have put the trip beyond the means of all but a few. It is very doubtful if the vessel ever used the existing small pier at Walton-on-the-Naze as the effective use of this pier was dependent on the state of the tide. More probably passengers were rowed to and from the ship by small beach boats, weather permitting! It is interesting to note that Walton Pier had been constructed in 1869 by the Walton-on-the-Naze Hotel and Pier Company of which Peter Bruff was a director.

In late 1888, The London, Woolwich and Clacton-on-Sea Steamboat Company made, what at first appears to be, an extraordinary decision. It was decided that the paddle steamer *Clacton* should be withdrawn from service and sold. She had been employed for one summer on the Thames and was a popular ship. At first it was assumed that the Company were not satisfied with the vessel and in a way

In July 1887, Hoboken *became the first 'deck saloon' paddle steamer to visit Great Yarmouth. This photograph, taken during the 1870s shows the vessel dressed overall and with a black funnel.*

The General Steam Navigation vessel Mavis *prepares to sail from Great Yarmouth. Just inside her is one of the other 'Classical Birds', probably the* Laverock.

is was true. She could not be described as a lucky ship, and certainly she had suffered some mechanical problems. Perhaps the most unfortunate incident occurred during the final trip of the season when she was struck by a tug while disembarking passengers at Blackwall. However, the annual report for 1888 reveals that *Clacton* was extremely successful and that a dividend of five per cent was payable to all shareholders. In fact *Clacton* was so successful that she proved to be too small for the potential traffic of the Clacton service. It was therefore recommended that a larger and faster vessel be acquired. In 1889 the *Clacton* was sold to a Mr. H. Surgondjie and was renamed *Aidin* before sailing to Turkey for use as a ferry on the Bosporus. There, her modern and probably temperamental engines caused the Turkish engineers numerous problems, so, to train them in the maintenance of this machinery, the Turkish Government employed, for a time, an English engineer. *Aidin* served as one of the notorious Bosporus ferries until she was withdrawn in 1913 and probably scrapped.

The Victoria Steamboat Association must have viewed the developments at Clacton with satisfaction. Here, surely, was an opportunity to expand further. For, unless the London, Woolwich and Clacton-on-Sea Steamboat Company could purchase a suitable steamer during the early months of 1889, they would be without a ship for the summer season. On the other hand, the Victoria Steamboat Association had vessels already available. The Directors of The London, Woolwich and Clacton-on-Sea Steamboat Company faced up to this problem in their own way and did not rush into any deals or mergers. Perhaps the mistakes they had made with the *Clacton* had made them cautious, for they waited patiently.

To cover the 1889 season an arrangement was made with the Victoria Steamboat Association that ensured a service to Clacton. This is just what the latter had wanted and while the *Glen Rosa* and *Alexandra* made regular appearances at Clacton their owners continued the search for new tonnage to meet the expected rise in demand for their services. This need became even greater when in September the *Alexandra* was wrecked near London Bridge, fortunately without loss of life.

Today, it is hard for us to conceive the number of people the developing East Coast resorts attracted. During peak summer weekends Clacton, Felixstowe, Lowestoft and Great Yarmouth were inundated with visitors. By 1889 one paddle steamer was completely insufficient to cope with the number of people arriving at the Thames boarding points and often two or three steamers were required to meet the demand. On more than one occasion I have found postcards on which people comment about the inability to get aboard steamers. At Great Yarmouth the 1889 August Bank Holiday Saturday saw twenty-one railway trains arrive at the Great Eastern Railway terminal; thirteen of these were Holiday Specials that were packed with visitors. At South Quay five General Steam Navigation Company ships arrived between 6.00 p.m. and 10.00 p.m., each full to capacity with 'human cargoes'. The vessels were recorded as being *Halcyon*, *Laverock*, *Hoboken*, *Swift*, and *Sir Walter Raleigh*. It is interesting to note that each Bank Holiday Saturday in the years 1887, 1888 and 1889 required an extra vessel to meet demand. So full was the town on Bank Holiday Saturday that by midnight families were still wandering around searching for accommodation and not surprisingly, considerable distress was witnessed on the streets. Long before breakfast on the Sunday, the beaches were already crowded. Lack of accommodation occasionally resulted in visitors attempting to reboard the steamer in search of shelter. On one occasion during 1889, a young gentleman on failing to find accommodation attempted to reboard the paddle steamer *Sir Walter Raleigh*. Unfortunately he was carrying a rather large portmanteau which caused him to lose his balance and fall into the swiftly flowing river. Luckily for him, his cries of help were heard by some passing coal heavers who went to his rescue. 'Coal heavers' was a term used to describe those men who worked long hours refilling the ships' bunkers from the railway trucks that were for many years a common feature on South Quay.

The arrival of the paddle steamers *Swift* and *Sir Walter Raleigh* at Great Yarmouth reveal just how stretched the General Steam Navigation were, even with the last two 'Classical Birds' entering service. Not only did the Company have to service the route to Great Yarmouth, which usually detained vessels overnight, but it had also to serve the equally busy Kent and Thanet routes. *Swift* and her sister vessel *Swallow* were the last paddle steamers purchased by the General Steam Navigation Company for use in other than the coastal holiday trade. Built on the Tees they had been purchased in 1875 for the Continental service. Although slow — the journey to Belgium took ten hours — they provided a regular service from St. Katharine's Wharf to Ostend right up until the turn of the century. In spite of their ungainly appearance they were said to be good seaboats with comfortable accommodation. *Sir Walter Raleigh* was a smaller vessel that had been built at Renfrew in 1862 and was usually found on Thames services. She continued to serve with General Steam Navigation until 1891 when she was withdrawn and sold.

Memories of the *Princss Alice* disaster ten years previously were revived briefly in August 1889, when the *Halcyon*, bound for Margate collided with a small tug named *Sunbeam* near Wapping. The tug was one of many used to move barges around the London docks. The bow of the crowded paddle steamer cut deeply into the *Sunbeam* causing her to capsize and sink almost immediately. Fortunately, her crew were thrown into the murky water to be rescued, dazed and shocked, amid much excitement by the passengers and the crew of the *Halcyon*. Later the paddle steamer, virtually unscathed, continued on its way. It was a timely reminder that the Thames was a busy, congested and potentially hazardous waterway. It was after all the arterial highway to the capital of the Empire.

During the early summer months of 1889 The London, Woolwich and Clacton-on-Sea Steamboat Company made a very significant move. They entered into negotiations with the ship-building company of William Denny & Brothers whose yards were on the Clyde at Dumbarton. On July 27th 1889 an order was placed with Denny's for a new paddle steamer to be delivered in 1890. So began a partnership between ship-builder and ship operator that would last well into the next century, for this vessel, order number 434, was due to be the first of the Belle Steamers. William Denny & Brothers were later to build all of the 'Belle' fleet and have a direct interest in the fortunes of their owners.

At about the same time that this vessel was taking shape on the Clyde, the Victoria Steamboat Association made a bold move that would ultimately change the very nature of Thames paddle steamers and give the general public a new dimension on which to make their judgements. They purchased from the Glasgow and Inveraray Company a paddle steamer named *Lord of the Isles*. She had been built in 1877 and has since been described as one of the most beautiful excursion steamers ever built. The standards of comfort expected on Clyde steamers had always been higher than anywhere else in Great Britain and it was not surprising that when *Lord of the Isles* appeared on the Thames, she attracted a great deal of public acclaim. Her upper deck reached just forward of the foremast giving a feeling of space, while her two funnels, one forward and one aft of the paddle boxes, presented a well-balanced appearance. The Victoria Steamboat Association adopted the colours of her former owners. These were a black hull with red funnels sporting three narrow bands, white, black and white near the top. Inside, the comfort afforded to passengers was unsurpassed by that of any other Thames steamer and so she established a precedent to which others would have to conform.

If the Belle Steamers can be said to have been 'born', then February 26th 1890 was their birthday. On that day representatives of the London, Woolwich and Clacton-on-Sea Steamboat Company assembled in the Dumbarton shipyard of William Denny to witness the launch of their new vessel. She was proudly named *Clacton Belle* and from the outset clearly rivalled any other paddle steamer on the Thames. A 246 foot long deck-saloon steamer, *Clacton Belle* had comfortable lounges, bars and two superbly equipped dining saloons. To enable her to pass under London Bridge to her mooring at Old Swan Pier, the single pole mast was hinged on a tabernacle so it could be lowered over the bow and the single funnel was telescopic. Manoeuvrability on the crowded Thames was enhanced by the addition of a bow rudder.

The close link between the builders and the owners is reflected in the contract details which strongly favoured the London, Woolwich and Clacton-on-Sea Steamboat Company. *Clacton Belle* was to reach eighteen miles per hour on a six hour trial and a penalty clause made Denny's liable to a payment of £250 for every tenth of a mile under that speed. To encourage the builders the Steamboat Company agreed to pay Denny's a bonus of £100 for every tenth of a mile over the guaranteed speed. The agreed price of £19,000 for the vessel was to be paid in four equal instalments of £3,000 while the ship was being built, and the remaining £7,000, in annual instalments of £1,000 at an interest rate of five percent. The London, Woolwich and Clacton-on-Sea Steamboat Company could reject the vessel if she failed to reach seventeen and a half miles per hour. Rejection was not unknown in paddle steamer construction where the intense competition experienced on certain routes necessitated a combination of comfort and speed. This combination not always easy to achieve as weight was critical. If the ship's displacement had not been accurately calculated, the paddle wheels could sit too low so that the paddle boxes would become clogged with water and inefficient. So great was the importance of design that sometimes builders went to great lengths to hide the identity of future owners from the industrial spies of the age. Less interest would be taken in a vessel bound for India than one for Scotland!

After successfully completing trials on the Clyde during April, *Clacton Belle* sailed for London on May 17th, and was immediately put on to her intended service to Clacton in direct competition with *Lord of the Isles* and *Glen Rosa*. *Clacton Belle* proved to be so successful that by September the London, Woolwich and Clacton-on-Sea Steamboat Company had decided to expand their routes north, to Walton, Harwich, Felixstowe and Ipswich. Both Walton-on-the-Naze and Felixstowe were developing as holiday resorts, while Ipswich was then a thriving market centre with a growing population. The long established Orwell packet service from London was run by the Victoria Steamboat Association's ageing *Fairy*

Queen (ex-*Queen of the Orwell*) and was therefore very vulnerable to competition. The London. Woolwich and Clacton-on-Sea Steamboat Company decided that a new vessel would be required for this route and, although it needed not to be as large as the *Clacton Belle*, it would nevertheless require all the facilities demanded by a discerning clientele. For shipbuilders, they looked no further than William Denny, and on 24th September 1890 they placed an order for a paddle steamer to be named *Woolwich Belle*.

By the end of 1890 the paddle steamer services along the East Coast were developing clear patterns. The large General Steam Navigation fleet, quite apart from dominating the services to Kent and the Continent, was running a direct London to Great Yarmouth return service using a variety of vessels. The Victoria Steamboat Association was running return services to Clacton, Harwich, Ipswich and the Kent resorts while the London, Woolwich and Clacton-on-Sea Steamboat Company, soon to be known to all as 'Belle Steamers', was becoming well established with their London to Clacton service and was poised to expand further.

Woolwich Belle was constructed during the winter of 1890/91 and was launched on April 6th 1891, by Abel Penfold's daughter. The contract for the *Woolwich Belle* clearly stated that she was to have a Board of Trade Certificate Number 3 for trading between Ipswich and Clacton during the months of April and October and to be ready for delivery in May 1891. On a six-hour trial she was to make seventeen and a quarter miles per hour but, as the Lennox *Herald* of May 16th 1891 reveals, she only just reached this guaranteed speed. As built, *Woolwich Belle* was some forty-six feet shorter than the *Clacton Belle* but bore some distinct similarities including the paddle box design, the telescopic funnel, the hinged mast and, as photographs of her show, the distinctive set of steps that led from the well deck to the promenade deck. Second class accommodation was placed forward while the first class was aft, both being provided with a wide range of facilities including comfortable dining rooms. Again, like the *Clacton Belle*, Denny's fitted out these dining rooms in a style that befitted the different classes; finest quality mahogany with decorated lincrusta panels in the first class saloon, while pine and paint were used for the second class saloon!

Woolwich Belle sailed from the Clyde on May 4th 1891 and arrived in time for the Spring Bank Holiday. However, she was not put onto her intended Orwell service but instead ran in partnership with *Clacton Belle* to Southend and Clacton. It had been found that there was enough demand on this route to warrant the use of both vessels and, it is also possible that berthing at Ipswich was something of a problem. So, it was from Old Swan Pier that *Woolwich Belle* began her career sailing daily to and from the Essex piers. It was a summer routine broken only by the occasional service to Gravesend and the busy port of Sheerness.

Fresh competition and the popularity of the *Lord of the Isles* with the London public, encouraged the Victoria Steamboat Association to seek an even more luxurious steamer. They decided to have built a vessel with a design based on the *Lord of the Isles* but of much greater size. To do this they entered into an unusual arrangement with the Glasgow ship-building and engineering company of Fairfields whose yards were not far from those of William Denny. The vessel would be built and mortgaged by Fairfields to the Victoria Steamboat Association, who would have complete control over its management. Fairfields already had shipping interests in North Wales, as the Liverpool and North Wales Steamship

Clacton Belle *on trials in the Clyde during April 1890. At this date the funnel was telescopic and painted black. It was later changed to a tall 'one piece' design and painted buff.*

An early view of the Woolwich Belle *showing her with a telescopic funnel. The photograph was probably taken after she commenced her services to Ipswich in 1894.*

Company was one of their subsidiaries and, in May 1891, they had delivered the new paddle steamer *St. Tudno* for service between Liverpool and Llandudno. Fairfields were now seeking new interests and the arrangement with the Victoria Steamboat Association was ideal as it would give them a financial interest in Thames steamboat services that would match their ship-building rivals at Dumbarton.

The new paddle steamer was named *Koh-i-Noor* after the famous diamond presented to Queen Victoria in 1850. Certainly this name was very apt for such a luxurious vessel as she was to be the 'jewel of the Thames' for many years and, as such, deserves detailed consideration. *Koh-i-Noor* was 310 feet in length and displaced 884 gross tons, almost twice the displacement of *Clacton Belle*. She had two large telescopic funnels that could be lowered by means of steam winches to enable her to pass under London Bridge while the single pole mast was hinged for the same purpose. She was constructed of steel to the highest specifications available and these included the recommendations of the Bulkheads Committee. Accordingly, she was divided into ten watertight compartments. One of these even transversed the first class saloon, effectively cutting it into two and necessitating special watertight doors to allow access! As befitting a ship of such dimensions she was given two rudders of unusual size. The one at the stern was nine feet long with a correspondingly large surface area, while the other, at the bow, was of a similar size but had been constructed so as to form an integral part of the stem. To power the vessel, *Koh-i-Noor* was equipped with massive diagonal compound engines sited forward of the paddle wheels. Her cylinders were placed side by side and were designed to develop 3,500 h.p. The High Pressure cylinder was forty-five inches, and the Low Pressure eighty inches in diameter! Steam was provided by four boilers working at a pressure of 120 lb/sq. in. To reach the working pressure each boiler required three furnaces which, not surprisingly, kept the crew very busy.

Probably the most outstanding feature of this ship was her promenade deck which extended for an uninterrupted three hundred feet from the stem almost to the stern. This was popular with passengers as it enabled them to stand right at the bow and watch the stem cleave through the water. The capstan and rope handling areas were situated below on the main deck. *Koh-i-Noor* was described by an observer writing soon after she entered service.

> "She has a spacious and well-ventilated saloon, beautifully upholstered in gold plush, the fittings being in solid mahogany, and is lighted at night by Swan-Edison electric lamps. This grand apartment, finished as it is with everything that comfort or luxury can suggest puts one in mind of a first class hotel drawing room, rather than a saloon on board a sea-going vessel. Beyond this, a special saloon is set apart as a ladies boudoir, and is finished in the same lavish style. Below the saloon are the fine suites of dining-rooms, with a capacity for dining about 200 persons at one sitting. A special feature of these rooms is the facility with which they can be divided, by means of a bulkhead compartment, into two separate saloons so as to provide additional safety in the event of danger, and, enabling the company to cater for large private parties which can have every privacy and attention, however large a number of general passengers may be on board.
>
> "Two galleys are fitted up with immense ranges, and are supplied with every requisite for cooking purposes, and are in constant operation. The cooks, under-stewards and waiters having a busy time of it during the hours allotted to the various meals.

"In wet weather there is covered accommodation on the *Koh-i-Noor* to the full extent of her licensed carrying power. For light-refreshment purposes there is a large bar for the use of those on deck at which beverages of all kinds can be procured at shore rates.

"Three state-rooms elaborately decorated and furnished occupy a position of the space allotted to the saloon and may be hired by small family parties, whilst sea baths, a shampooing room and other arrangements for the enjoyment of passengers are provided".

As the reader may conclude, she was a very imposing vessel and was likely to be a great threat to the London, Woolwich and Clacton-on-Sea Steamboat Company's services to Clacton.

However commodious *Koh-i-Noor* may have been, the sea is fickle and fate almost prevented her from entering service. After successfully completing trials during which her speed had been measured at 19.49 knots, *Koh-i-Noor* left the Clyde on May 23rd 1892 bound for London. Soon after leaving, the weather deteriorated and her Captain decided to make for Belfast Lough. There she remained for two days until the weather abated and on May 26th she passed through the Irish Sea. Later that night, while off St. David's Head she encountered thick fog and wisely slowed down, proceeding cautiously until a grinding crunch brought her to a sudden halt. She had run herself onto rocks off Porthgain Head and had severely damaged her bows. After making sure that the remaining watertight compartments were secure, *Koh-i-Noor* teased herself from the rock's grasp and with a tug in attendance gently made her way towards Milford Haven. The first two watertight bulkheads had collapsed and the third bulged ominously. The water flooding in had increased her forward draught by four feet, completely upsetting her trim. It was only when she had arrived on the "gridiron" and the tide had receded that the full extent of the damage could be seen. About twenty feet of her bows had been crushed rather like a concertina but, surprisingly not a plate had been cracked! The giant rudder and the bulkheads had to a large extent taken the force and probably saved the ship. It was decided to return *Koh-i-Noor* to the Clyde after temporary repairs had been carried out. Once back at Govan the damaged bow was removed in one piece and a new one constructed and fitted in just six days! After further trials *Koh-i-Noor* arrived in London on July 2nd and the following day entered service with a run to Clacton and Harwich. This arrangement allowed the Victoria Steamboat Association more flexibility and so in mid July *Glen Rosa* left the Thames for a summer charter to the Hastings, St. Leonards and Eastbourne Steamboat Company.

The arrival of *Koh-i-Noor* prompted the London, Woolwich and Clacton-on-Sea Steamboat Company to order another vessel to match her for speed and comfort. An order was placed with Denny's on August 29th 1892, for a ship to be delivered in time for the 1893 season. The contract drawn up specifically stated that the new vessel was to be designed so as "to beat" the rival Victoria Steamboat Association's *Koh-i-Noor*. As for the summer of 1892 the rival Companies entered a period of intense competition. Their steamers left Old Swan Pier for Clacton at the same time as those of the Victoria Steamboat Association and, although officially discouraged, racing was a regular occurrence. This caused great excitement amongst the passengers and much consternation on the part of the river authorities. In June 1892, Captain Alexander Owen of the *Koh-i-Noor* was fined five pounds for racing his vessel against the *Clacton Belle* but, occasionally, the outcome of such races was even more surprising! In the previous year, a race between *Woolwich Belle* and *Lord of the Isles* culminated in the latter colliding with Clacton Pier, causing substantial damage to the pier structure and to the vessel. With his ship immobilised, Captain Prior requested assistance and the *Woolwich Belle* was pleased to oblige! She towed her rival to a safe anchorage from which, two days later, *Lord of the Isles* was towed away for repairs. Further complaints were to be made about racing before, in September 1892, the two Companies agreed upon a simple compromise. The Companies' vessels were timetabled to leave London piers first on alternate mornings! But, by the end of the summer season the impact made by *Koh-i-Noor* on the Thames passenger services was so great that the London, Woolwich and Clacton-on-Sea Steamboat Company could only look on enviously and await their new vessel.

It is unlikely that the Victoria Steamboat Association knew exactly what the London, Woolwich and Clacton-on-Sea Steamboat Company's plans were. Denny's could be very secretive, especially when rival ship-builders were concerned. In 1890 they had constructed the paddle steamer *Duchess of Hamilton* for the Caledonian Steam Packet Company but in order to conceal the identity of her intended owners it was announced that the vessel was being constructed for use in Australian waters. Her name was given as *Ozone* or *Australia* and her owners as Martin and Williamson. It was not until a few weeks before her launch that the press announced the totally artificial ''sale'' of the vessel to the Caledonian Steam Packet Company. Incidentally, the *Koh-i-Noor* was equipped with a promenade deck similar to that of *Duchess of Hamilton* and it has been suggested that Fairfields copied the design.

Koh-i-Noor had been so successful in her first season that it was decided to order a sister vessel for the 1893 season. Whatever move was made by the London. Woolwich and Clacton-on-Sea Company, this would enable the Victoria Steamboat Association to keep one step ahead of their rivals along the Essex coast and give them more flexibility on services to Kent. It was also hoped that the presence of such vessels would convince the Thames Conservancy of the need to improve their river piers. The condition of these had, in some cases deteriorated to the point of concern. Certainly they did not match the luxury of the vessels that used them or the demands of their clientele. Also, it was hoped that further restrictions would be placed on barge owners whose groups of moored lighters were causing navigational problems to the larger steamers. This was especially so in the upper reaches of the Thames where the steamer's position had to be exact in order to clear the bridges.

The General Steam Navigation Company viewed the developments of 1891 and 1892 with concern but no apparent alarm. They were quite prepared to continue their services using their existing ships, and in 1891 had even decided to dismantle some of their older vessels including *Sir Walter Raleigh* and *Seine.*

Those who anticipated that 1893 was to be an eventful year for East Coast paddle steamers were not to be disappointed. Not only did the year witness the appearance of the London, Woolwich and Clacton-on-Sea Steamboat Company's new vessel named *London Belle*, the *Koh-i-Noor*'s sister, named *Royal Sovereign*, but rather unexpectedly, it also saw the establishment of a service that threatened the General Steam Navigation Company's monopoly on the route to Great Yarmouth.

The threat came, as might have been expected, from the ambitious Victoria Steamboat Association but, surprisingly it took the form of the ageing *Glen Rosa* which had returned from a charter at the end of 1892 and was to a large extent 'spare tonnage'. It was decided to use her to establish a service to Great Yarmouth in July. It must be said that there was an air of scepticism, and it was stated in the press that it would not be possible to complete the voyage from Old Swan Pier to Great Yarmouth in one day, if the anticipated stops were made at Clacton and Harwich. However, the writer does say that a route which allowed voyagers to visit places of interest would have its advocates especially as the fares were "exceedingly reasonable".

Obviously the Victoria Steamboat Association had not published the exact form that the service would take. They did not intend to run *Glen Rosa* from London but instead to use *Koh-i-Noor*'s existing daily service to Harwich and send *Glen Rosa* from Great Yarmouth to meet her. From the Company's point of view this was very sensible as *Koh-i-Noor* under the command of Captain Owen had built up a considerable reputation. While, from Great Yarmouth's viewpoint, having *Glen Rosa* based in the port would also benefit the town as the ship would need local caterers and fuel suppliers.

The General Steam Navigation Company were slow to respond to this challenge. They had opened their summer service in mid-June but only on a bi-weekly basis! They seemed content to continue in the way of previous years using the older *Hoboken* as the mainstay of the service. Their complacency was probably based on the fact that they had brought visitors to the port for twenty-seven years and during that time not one passenger had suffered an accident. The reason for this achievement was, according to the press, that the Company possessed "competent, genial Captains and capable seamen". This claim did not influence the Victoria Steamboat Association and *Glen Rosa* duly arrived in Great Yarmouth on the evening of July 1st with about a hundred passengers aboard. She moored at Crane Quay not far from her rivals and for the rest of the season her sailings were widely advertised. She left each day, except Friday, at 10.00 a.m. bound for Harwich where she arrived at 2.00 p.m. At Ha'penny Pier she exchanged passengers with *Koh-i-Noor* which then returned to London. *Glen Rosa* immediately left for Great Yarmouth where she docked at about 7.30 p.m., the journey time from London being about eleven hours. A fact not widely advertised was that *Glen Rosa*'s journey was not always made without stopping. At Lowestoft an arrangement was made with a boat owner named David Cook to ferry passengers, weather permitting, to a point off the harbour mouth where he would meet *Glen Rosa* and transfer passengers. Knowing the North Sea, the transhipment of Victorian ladies and gentlemen complete with their luggage must have been quite a spectacle. It may seem strange but I can find no record of any mishaps!

By late July the attitude of the General Steam Navigation Company had changed. Each day advertisements appeared in the press announcing that they were the "original and favourite line to London", adding that, "passengers by this line do not have to change boats". By mid-August they were regularly employing 'Classical Birds' on the service. On the Saturday prior to the Summer Bank Holiday, over two thousand passengers disembarked from five General Steam Navigation Company vessels. Trade was certainly brisk as the Victoria Steamboat Association were also doing "big business in the London passenger Traffic". *Glen Rosa* ran her final return service on September 18th and the following day set out for London direct.

The luxurious Lord of the Isles *had originally been built for Clyde services in 1877. When she first appeared on the Thames she outclassed any other paddle steamer on the river and it is not surprising that she became a great favourite with London passengers.*

Earlier in the year, on March 10th, Denny's had launched their rival to *Koh-i-Noor*. She was named *London Belle* by Miss Penfold and was the first *Belle* Steamer to be fitted with the more efficient diagonal triple expansion engines. On trials during late April she had reached a speed of 19.405 knots between the Cloch and Cumbrae lighthouses. This was slightly less than the larger *Koh-i-Noor* but, as the sea conditions were said to have been very unfavourable for such trials, her speed was thought to be "eminently satisfactory". *London Belle* was to be the largest vessel in the *Belle* fleet with a length of 280 feet and a displacement of 787 gross tons. Other features included eight watertight bulkheads and a newly invented 'spark catcher' which was fitted to the funnel. During the previous year sparks had set fire to the canvas awning on *Koh-i-Noor*, a mishap which could so easily have had tragic consequences. *London Belle* was constructed to a pattern closely followed by all the subsequent *Belle* Steamers. The first class lounge and dining saloon were placed aft of the paddle boxes and stretched across the full width of the ship. The lounge was rather short but well fitted out with mahogany tables and chairs upholstered in velvet plush. Good sea views were provided by the large rectangular windows that ran along both sides, while stewards provided for the various needs of the passengers from a well-equipped galley and bar. At the stern, the last part of the main deck was covered by an awning which allowed first class passengers some sheltered external accommodation on sunny days. The second class saloon was situated forward of the paddle boxes but did not extend across the full width of the vessel's main deck. Along each side was a passage covered by the promenade deck which afforded second class passengers a degree of shelter and access to the open well deck forward. The promenade deck extended the full width of the ship and provided a comfortable, if at times a windswept vantage point from which to view the surroundings. *London Belle* may not have had the rather ostentatious flamboyance of *Koh-i-Noor*, but she was fast, well-equipped and probably a better seaboat than her rival. *London Belle* sailed from the Clyde on May 12th 1893 and on Saturday May 20th commenced services to Clacton and Harwich in competition with *Koh-i-Noor*. During August *London Belle* terminated its run at Clacton, so it might have been that the competition to Harwich was too great or, more probably, that her owners decided that the vessel would be more gainfully employed returning to London before *Koh-i-Noor* returned to Clacton from Harwich.

At this date the London, Woolwich and Clacton-on-Sea Steamboat Company ceased to use the Old Swan Pier and moved their departure point to Fresh Wharf, called by the General Steam Navigation Company, "London Bridge Wharf". Given the awkward position of Old Swan Pier this move was probably long overdue! It was for this reason that *London Belle* had not been equipped with a telescopic funnel. However, she did have a hinged foremast which could be lowered over the bow, enabling the vessel to manoeuvre right under the arches of London Bridge, thus saving space at the already very busy pier.

The change of piers also allowed for modifications to be made to *Clacton Belle*. Her telescopic funnel was replaced by one rather akin to that of *London Belle*, while at the same time her promenade deck was lengthened and a longer second class saloon created underneath. This certainly enhanced both her appearance and her facilities.

The facilities provided by the London, Woolwich and Clacton-on-Sea Steamboat

The first class lounge of the London Belle *was electrically lit and sumptuously finished in rich mahogany and velvet. It was here that stewards were kept busy catering for the demands made by a discerning clientele.*

One of the few surviving photographs that show the inside of a Belle Steamer. This is the magnificent first class dining saloon of the Clacton Belle.

Company were to be of increasing importance as only two days before *London Belle*'s inaugural trip to Clacton, the Victoria Steamboat Association's new vessel arrived in the Thames after the quickest maiden passage on record from the Clyde. Named *Royal Sovereign*, she had been built by Fairfields as a near sister to *Koh-i-Noor* and as such had all the luxury of the earlier vessel. Apart from being fractionally larger, *Royal Sovereign* possessed what has been described as "a much improved profile". This was simply achieved by positioning the funnels twelve feet further forward than those of *Koh-i-Noor*. Like her near sister, *Royal Sovereign* was mortgaged from her builders by Palace Steamers Ltd., best regarded as a subsidiary company of the Victoria Steamboat Association, who in practice managed the vessel. *Royal Sovereign* was put into service to the Kent resorts leaving Old Swan Pier at 9.30 a.m. and calling at Greenwich, South Woolwich and Tilbury before reaching Margate at 1.45 p.m. and Ramsgate at 2.25 p.m. She returned by the same route arriving back at London Bridge at 8.05 p.m. *Royal Sovereign* was to spend most of her working life on the Kent services and from the outset she was a great favourite with Londoners. She is reputed to have been the "best loved of all Thames paddle steamers". By chance, *London Belle* and *Royal Sovereign* both made their maiden passenger-paying trips on the same day, leaving their respective piers at the same time! It must have been quite an occasion to have been standing on London Bridge.

1893 marked the zenith of the Victoria Steamboat Association, for 1894 was to prove a season of mixed fortunes. It all started well in June when they acquired what was probably the ultimate in paddle steamer design: *La Marguerite*. Arnold Williams, the ambitious manager of the Association, had long foreseen that services to the Continent were in need of up-dating. If the luxury of *Koh-i-Noor* could be introduced to that service then his Company would dominate the market, a market so long the prerogative of the General Steam Navigation Company. It was to meet this need that Fairfields built *La Marguerite* to the order of Palace Steamers. Named after Arnold Williams' daughter, she was an enormous ship, 330 feet in length and 40 feet across the beam. Only one larger paddle steamer was to operate in British waters, that being the Isle of Man Steam Packet Company's *Empress Queen*. To power the ship she was equipped with two-cylinder compound diagonal engines designed by Fairfield's engineering director, Andrew Laing. These drove her at speeds of over twenty-one knots. Although she resembled *Koh-i-Noor* as regards internal luxury, the deck arrangements were rather different in that her size allowed an extra deck to be incorporated, this being known as the "upper deck". It ran the entire length of the vessel and was plated down to the main deck directly below so as to give *La Marguerite* a high freeboard. Consequently she was a much drier seaboat than any of her General Steam Navigation rivals. The promenade deck was placed on top of the upper deck and extended for three quarters of the vessel's length, but, unlike *Royal Sovereign* or *Koh-i-Noor*, it did not stretch to the bow.

Everything on board was of giant proportions and unfortunately, this also included her coal bill! Not that this worried her passengers who paid a mere ten shillings and sixpence in London for a return trip to Boulogne. Her well-patronised services ran initially from Blackwall and it was to here that small tenders ran from many of the up-river piers each morning. At Tilbury, rail passengers from Fenchurch Street were embarked prior to the vessel leaving the

Koh-i-Noor is pictured leaving Harwich Ha'penny Pier. It was from Harwich that the Victoria Steamboat Association extended their services to Great Yarmouth during 1893/94.

This postcard of Edwardian Margate shows clearly one of the major differences between Royal Sovereign *on the left, and* Koh-i-Noor *on the right. The funnels of* Royal Sovereign *had been set some twelve feet further forward than those of her sister, and this resulted in her having a more balanced profile.*

41

Thames. After a short stop at Margate, *La Marguerite* left for Boulogne which was reached five and a half hours after leaving London. However, she was never far from controversy, and even in the wide lower reaches of the Thames numerous complaints were made concerning her wash. Not being a vessel that was used along the East Coast it is enough to say here that although popular, it is doubtful whether *La Marguerite* was profitable. She was more likely a drain on the Victoria Steamboat Association's funds.

The London, Woolwich and Clacton-on-Sea Steamboat Company may not have owned such a magnificent vessel, but nevertheless, they had made a significant move when on 12th May 1894, in atrocious weather, they had opened their long awaited Orwell services. *Woolwich Belle*, initially under the command of Samuel Mason, late of the *Bonnie Doon*, sailed daily, Fridays excepted, from the New Lock Gates at Ipswich to Clacton, arriving in time to meet the London boat. An agreement had been made with the Great Eastern Railway whereby *Woolwich Belle* was able to use the piers at Harwich (Ha'penny) and Felixstowe (Riverside). However, she could only embark passengers on the way out and disembark them on her return. By forbidding *Woolwich Belle* to compete with their existing Orwell vessels, the Great Eastern Railway protected its interests and made a handsome profit. The trial trip made on 10th May was quite a celebration with dignitaries from both Ipswich and from the vessel's owners aboard. *Woolwich Belle* was to remain based at Ipswich for the next fifteen years and was to become so much a part of the dockland scene that she was once described as ''Ipswich's number one amenity''.

In July 1894 the Victoria Steamboat Association returned to Great Yarmouth with yet another new paddle steamer named *Victoria*. She was a larger and more modern vessel than *Glen Rosa*, and with two funnels in some-ways resembled *Lord of the Isles*. *Victoria*, was yet another Scottish exile. She had been built in 1886 by Blackwood and Gordon at Glasgow for use on the Clyde and from these waters she had moved on to do charter work in Ireland and South Wales before being purchased by the London and East Coast Steamship Company in 1894. This latter Company is another of those best regarded as a Victoria Steamboat Association subsidiary, as, like Palace Steamers, the Association managed all its affairs. The service provided by the *Victoria* was the same as that of *Glen Rosa* in 1893, passengers being transferred to *Koh-i-Noor* at Harwich. Although these two vessels were much more compatible as regards size and luxury, the service got off to an inauspicious start when the portable ticket office being carried to Great Yarmouth was accidentally dropped from *Victoria*'s deck on to the quay, seriously injuring a stevedore.

As in the previous year, the General Steam Navigation responded to the challenge by a campaign of press advertisements which stressed that they ran a direct service for the same price! Again they relied heavily on the *Hoboken* and their fleet of 'Classical Birds' while only occasionally using older 'Continental' steamers.

Over the August Bank Holiday *Victoria* broke her mainmast but just how this happened I've not discovered, anyway, this was a relatively small matter compared with what happened to the Association a week later. On August 8th, a petition was presented to the Chancery Court by the engineering company, Robinson and Dodd of Poplar, in respect of four thousand pounds owed to them for repairs to Association vessels. Although the resulting Court order enabled the

The power and size of La Marguerite *is clearly seen in this early view of the vessel. Although popular, she was never profitable on the cross-channel service for London.*

Glen Rosa *approaches Margate Jetty at about 6.00pm on a summer day in 1894.* La Marguerite *has just left for London while the P.S.* India, *distinguished by two funnels, also approaches the pier.*

Association to continue to trade, their finances were in turmoil. During the Autumn, Fairfields foreclosed their mortgages on the three prestigious steamers; *Koh-i-Noor*, *Royal Sovereign* and *La Marguerite*, and repossessed them. The enormous investments made during the previous seasons had been too much for the Association's financial stability. But The London, Woolwich and Clacton-on-Sea Steamboat Company had no intention of making the same mistakes; instead they quietly consolidated their position and like the General Steam Navigation waited to see what would happen next.

If the London, Woolwich and Clacton-on-Sea Steamboat Company had thought they had seen the last of the Victoria Steamboat Association they were mistaken, for their rivals still maintained ownership of a fleet that included *Lord of the Isles*, *Glen Rosa* and *Victoria*. In 1895 these three vessels appeared for the summer season running a much reduced service with more emphasis on Kent than on Essex. *Lord of the Isles* ran to Clacton, while *Glen Rosa* was sent to Rochester. Without *Koh-i-Noor* the Great Yarmouth connection was discontinued and *Victoria* was put on the run to Southend and Margate. This service brought her into competition with *Royal Sovereign* for, rather than sell their three Thames vessels, Fairfields had formed a new company under the title 'New Palace Steamers', a name which must not be confused with the Association's earlier "Palace Steamers". The three Fairfield vessels provided a service much as before, with *Royal Sovereign* running along the Thanet coast, *Koh-i-Noor* running the Clacton service and *La Marguerite* going to Boulogne. Indeed, the most noticeable change was that the funnels had been painted buff. The extension from Clacton to Harwich was not advertised as it had been in previous years and was confined to Saturdays, Sundays and Mondays. The emphasis of the new company's Essex services was centred on Clacton, for, as the London, Woolwich and Clacton-on-Sea Steamboat Company had found previously, it was on this route that the profit was to be found.

The London, Woolwich and Clacton-on-Sea Steamboat Company's services for 1895 were almost identical with those of the previous year, the only hiccup being early in the season when *Woolwich Belle* was suddenly, and without explanation, withdrawn from Ipswich. Initial concern was soon dispelled when it became clear that she was only temporarily required in London to replace *London Belle* which had suffered a serious mechanical breakdown. By early August she was back running her usual service which now included a wide range of excursions. Two of the most popular were a sea trip to Orford Ness and a "Moonlight Trip" down the Orwell and out to sea.... weather permitting! One other interesting item of news had occurred in June when *London Belle* and *Koh-i-Noor* had found themselves together in the Thames both *en route* to Clacton. In the unofficial race that commenced *London Belle* reached the pier first much to the delight of her owners. The specifications outlined in her original contract had been fulfilled.

In the closing months of 1895 the London, Woolwich and Clacton-on-Sea Steamboat Company decided that there was room for the further expansion of their services. The Victoria Steamboat Association's declining fortunes had left a vacuum that, with care, could be profitably filled. Accordingly, plans for another vessel were drawn up with William Denny & Brothers of Dumbarton, and on 25th October 1895 an order was placed for a new paddle steamer of an intermediate size between that of *London Belle* and *Clacton Belle*. The contract stated that she was to have a Board of Trade number three certificate for trading between London and Harwich during the months April to October. As an indication of their future plans it also stated that she was to be capable of trading to Great Yarmouth as well. The Victoria Steamboat Association had shown that the volume of passenger traffic to Great Yarmouth warranted the competition with the General Steam Navigation Company which such a service would involve. It is conceivable that they also coveted the Thanet service that had been dominated by *Royal Sovereign* since 1893. According to the local Margate press, this vessel alone regularly landed upward of fifteen hundred passengers at the jetty! On 27th December the company directors called an Extraordinary General Meeting at Clacton, where it was decided that with the impending expansion a reconstruction of the company was necessary to attract more capital. By this date the Company chairman, Abel Penfold, had become very influential. He was a London County Councillor, a Woolwich wine merchant, and, it may be remembered, had been one of the businessmen who had taken an early interest in Clacton during the 1870s, through the involvement of the Woolwich Steam Packet Company. On 3rd February he chaired the meeting at which the company was retitled 'Belle Steamers Limited' and it is recorded that of their initial (1887) 10,000 share issue approximately half had been taken up. From this date on, the company developed rapidly.

The company's new vessel, was named *Southend Belle* by Miss Spence, daughter of Horace Spence, the company secretary, on Wednesday 6th March 1896. The ship closely resembled other members of the fleet being of that "graceful mould" that typified a Denny paddle steamer. The 249 feet long vessel was fitted with direct acting, triple diagonal surface-condensing engines, steam being provided by two navy-type boilers working at a pressure of 160 pounds to the square inch. As to be expected, *Southend Belle* was luxuriously fitted out. On the main deck there was a handsome first class saloon, the entrance to which was gained through stained glass doors engraved with the Company's crest. Polished sycamore abounded along the sides where square windows, curtained in blue and gold, allowed good sea views. In the centre of the ceiling was a beautiful saddle-backed skylight filled and tinted with 'cathedral glass'. The saloon was divided into a number of small bays with tables and chairs upholstered in blue frieze velvet. A number of portable ottomans finished off the air of elegance created. At the entrance to the saloon was the 'ladies boudoir' edged in dark mahogany. Even the adjoining toilet was upholstered in peacock blue! Below the saloon, on the lower deck, and reached by means of a double staircase decorated with stained glass that depicted the four seasons, was the first class dining room capable of seating 120 passengers. This was upholstered in gold 'Utrecht' velvet with matching gold curtains and framed in polished sycamore panelled in lincrusta. As in *Koh-i-Noor*, the dining room was divided by a watertight bulkhead and door. Thoughtfully, an emergency escape ladder was provided in case the door needed to be closed! For those wishing to travel in even more style the builders provided two private sitting rooms fitted out in walnut and pine. Like all the modern ships then being built, *Southend Belle* was fitted with electric light, some sixty-three lamps being installed.

Abel Penfold was aboard the vessel when she ran her trials early in May and he must have been well-pleased to see the ship exceed expectations by making 18.42 knots on the Cloch-Cumbrae run. In an after-dinner speech made aboard *Southend Belle* as she returned to the shipyard following the final trial, Penfold told the assembled dignitaries that "the *Belle* Company had come to stay" and that it was his intention to purchase only the very best vessels available. In short, he made it clear that he was determined to put his Company in the front rank of paddle steamer travel.

By the time *Southend Belle* entered service in May 1896, the *Belle* Steamers had achieved a virtual monopoly along the east coast. Earlier in the year New Palace Steamers had announced that *Koh-i-Noor* would no longer run a service to the Essex resorts but would instead partner *Royal Sovereign* on the Kent services. This decision put great presssure on the General Steam Navigation Company who by now had a monopoly only on the service to Great Yarmouth.

Apart from one mishap off Felixstowe, when an engineer accidentally disabled the vessel, *Southend Belle* proved to be very successful and a great favourite with passengers and crew. She became the first *Belle* steamer to visit Great Yarmouth when, during August 1896, she arrived in the port on an excursion with the families of Company employees aboard. Certainly *Southend Belle* influenced the Company's future planning, for on 8th October 1896 they placed yet another order with William Denny's for a similar, but slightly smaller paddle steamer, that was equipped with the same Board of Trade certificate. It was with this new vessel that *Belle* Steamers intended to extend their services to Great Yarmouth in 1897.

Any lingering threat posed by the Victoria Steamboat Association had ceased by 1897. During the previous Autumn the decision had been taken to sell *Lord of the Isles*, *Victoria* and *Glen Rosa*, and keep only their up-river fleet of small vessels. Of the trio only *Lord of the Isles* was to remain on the Thames. She was sold to Mr. P. B. Black and registered in the name of Mrs. C. Black. P.B. Black had been the Superintending Naval Architect for Palace Steamers and was therefore closely linked to the Victoria Steamboat Association. Perhaps this connection is why the vessel was registered in his wife's name. *Victoria* was purchased by Clyde Steamers Ltd. and in June 1897 returned to her native Scotland. During that summer she became notorious as a 'Sabbath Breaker' along the Clyde and references to her are often found in newspapers south of the border. Unfortunately, her career was brought to a premature end after only one season, when she was gutted by fire at Broomielaw. *Glen Rosa* was sold, rather surprisingly considering her age and reputation, to shipowner Alexander Campbell and so, after sixteen years, *Glen Rosa* left the Thames for Bristol. At times her career may have been eventful, even dramatic, but we must not forget those early years in the previous decade when it was *Glen Rosa* which inaugurated routes and set standards. The part she played in our story has, in the past, often been neglected and certainly, under estimated.

When other ships of her age were being dismantled, *Glen Rosa* embarked on a new career. In 1898 she came under the control of P. & A. Campbell Ltd. Within a short time she had become well known to the crowds that thronged the south coast and Bristol Channel. She soldiered on, after considerable 'modernisation', until 1914 when she was laid up in Bristol. In 1915 and again in 1916, she was used to maintain the important Cardiff to Weston-super-Mare ferry service. Then, in May 1917, at the age of forty years, *Glen Rosa* hoisted the white ensign and went to war. Requisitioned by the Admiralty for mine-sweeping duties, she joined the 17th Mine-sweeping Flotilla at Portland and in this role she served in the Bristol Channel and later, the Thames. She survived these hazardous duties and in May 1919 was returned to her owners at Bristol. However, the rigours of the previous five years had put her beyond economical reconditioning and she was again laid up to linger on, gradually deteriorating, until in 1921 she was sold to the ship-breaking firm of Pugsley who dismantled her at Bristol.

On April 5th 1897 *Belle* Steamer's new vessel was named *Walton Belle* at Dumbarton. At 230 feet, she was slightly shorter than *Southend Belle* but, as April progressed, she was fitted out with the same sumptuous luxury as that of her predecessor. *Walton Belle* had her hull divided into nine watertight compartments which prompted the Dumbarton Herald to comment that this division ''would practically secure her from foundering under any circumstances''. The first class saloon was very similar to that of the *Southend Belle* except that it was finished in oak and sycamore with paint and gilding that ''harmonised with these lighter woods''. The chairs and sofas, upholstered in blue frieze velvet, were deliberately arranged so as to give a warm ''home-like'' appearance. The dining saloons were fitted out in yellow pine with matching paintwork and were situated below the main deck. Both first and second class passengers were to be well-catered for by the well-equipped galley situated between the saloons. *Walton Belle*'s final price was £21,859 12s 6d, giving Denny Brothers a profit of £911 12s 6d.

On trials between the Cloch and Cumbrae lighthouses, *Walton Belle* reached a mean speed of 17.09 knots, just over half a knot greater than the speed she had been contracted to reach and this pleased all concerned, especially her owners. Indeed, during a trip up Loch Long to Arrochar, the company chairman, Abel Penfold, paid a great compliment to the builders when he said that from experience, his Company should be quite prepared to take steamers from Messrs Denny ''without the formality of trials''. Penfold went on to announce that although the *Walton Belle* had been ordered for the London to Clacton service, she was instead going to initiate a new service between Clacton and Great Yarmouth. On May 28th *Walton Belle* left the Clyde for London where she arrived a few days later after a very rough passage.

On June 2nd the local newspapers at Great Yarmouth announced that *Belle* Steamers were to extend their services to Yarmouth from Clacton using their ''new saloon steamer *Walton Belle*. She duly arrived on the evening of Saturday June 5th with flags flying, to be greeted by hundreds of townsfolk on the quayside. A few days later a sea trip was arranged for the benefit of local dignitaries from Yarmouth and Norwich. During a sumptuous dinner somewhere off Corton, Abel Penfold stated that he ''believed that there was good business to be done between Yarmouth and London'' and in a direct reference to the earlier service provided by the Victoria Steamboat Association, he said that he saw his company ''endeavouring to resuscitate'' that trade. Penfold referred to the General Steam Navigation Company as ''friendly rivals'' and stated that he did not wish to seem ''antagonistic'' towards them but, in the next breath, he referred to them as having ''indifferent passenger steamers''. *Belle* Steamers, he maintained, were determined from the first to keep up their high standards. They didn't know what it was to be beaten, in fact, the word was not to be found in (his) Company's vocabulary''.

Throughout her first season *Walton Belle* was under the command of Captain Prior who, it may be remembered, had been in command of the *Lord of the Isles* when she collided with Clacton Pier. To my knowledge he never repeated this manoeuvre but, instead, quickly established a routine similar to that developed by the Victoria Steam boat Association in late 1894. *Walton Belle* would sail daily from

The "Walton Belle."

Walton Belle *leaves Walton for Great Yarmouth. This was one of a series of photographs taken of* Belle *Steamers from Walton Pier and was probably sold aboard the vessel.*

A photograph, probably taken on a busy weekend in Great Yarmouth, shows Southend Belle *preparing to sail, while* Walton Belle *awaits her passengers.*

Great Yarmouth at 9.30 a.m., Friday excepted, for Clacton and, as in 1894, a brief stop was made off Lowestoft harbour to enable passengers to transfer to and from David Cook's yawls. The vessel arrived off Clacton at about 2.00 p.m. and passengers had the choice of spending a short time ashore or transferring to the London boat which returned to the Fresh Wharf via Southend and Gravesend. The exact time of *Walton Belle*'s departure from Clacton was dependent upon the arrival of the London boat. On the latter's arrival, Clacton Pier would become a hive of activity with *London Belle* (London to Clacton) disembarking, while *Woolwich Belle* (from Ipswich and Harwich) and *Walton Belle* (for Great Yarmouth) were both laying off, waiting their turn to use the solitary berth at the pier head. After loading, the *Walton Belle* would leave the pier for Lowestoft and Great Yarmouth, arriving in the Yare at about 6.30 p.m. to moor overnight at Hall Quay just downstream from the General Steam Navigation Company's berth.

The General Steam Navigation Company's response to this challenge to their last monopoly was an advertising campaign similar to that seen in 1893. They stressed "reasonable prices" and between July 5th and 24th significantly reduced their fares:

London to Great Yarmouth direct 4/- single.

6/- return.

These prices were so reasonable that I doubt if any profit was made! This effort to boost trade was really not surprising as the General Steam Navigation Company were once again being faced with a dilemma. With the exception of *Hoboken*, it was not that their vessels were particularly old, it was simply that they were slow and out of date when compared with other Thames steamers. Indeed, none of them had electric lights! The 'Classical Birds' were outclassed in every respect by the *Walton Belle* on the Great Yarmouth run, just as they were to Kent by the New Palace Steamers. To make matters worse, General Steam Navigation were censured by the Great Yarmouth Port and Haven Commissioners for the decline in income from steamer traffic. It had been openly stated at a meeting in June 1897 that it was "to be hoped that the General Steam Navigation would endeavour to increase their trade so that the Commissioners could recoup their losses". The General Steam Navigation Company's choice was quite simple; it was the same as they had experienced in 1885. Either they were to run at a loss or they had to invest in new tonnage. They decided on the latter and ordered a replacement for old *Hoboken* from Gourlay Brothers of Dundee. This new paddle steamer, named *Eagle*, was to be delivered in the summer of 1898. She was the first of the famous "Eagle Steamers" that were to be so popular on the Thames for over half a century.

General Steam Navigation's need for new tonnage was aggravated during the summer of 1897 by the regular appearance of *Southend Belle* on the fiercely competitive Margate service. She was advertised as running an "Express Service" direct from Fresh Wharf, leaving at 10.00 a.m. and returning from Margate later that evening. The return trip was broken at Tilbury, giving passengers the opportunity to save time by catching a train into London. On Saturdays *Southend Belle* was employed as the "Husbands' Boat". This strange title refers to husbands who, finishing work at mid-day, wished to join their families for the rest of the weekend in the resorts of Kent or Essex. The popular "Husbands' Boats" were often filled to capacity with workers flush with money and so were very profitable.

Southend Belle left Fresh Wharf at 2.00 p.m., calling at Tilbury at 2.50 p.m. where her arrival coincided with that of a special boat train from Fenchurch Street. The crowded steamer reached Margate at about 6.30 p.m. and returned to London shortly afterwards.

The arrival of *Belle* Steamers at Margate in 1897, was almost certainly the result of the demise of the Victoria Steamboat Association Palace Steamers, whose vessels had been sold during the year. Previously, in *Southend Belles's* first season, 1896, both the Palace Steamer's remaining vessels had been employed running to Margate from Old Swan Pier and for *Southend Belle* to have added to the competition would have been financially unwise for *Belle* Steamers. This new service to Kent did not tempt *Belle* Steamers to venture across the channel, although they now had the ships for this service. Instead, and probably in the event wisely, they left these journeys to New Palace Steamers and their vessels *La Belgique*, bought second hand that season, and *La Marguerite*, now running from Tilbury and under the command of Alexander Owen. Under Penfold's chairmanship the *Belle* Steamers had now developed an extensive network of routes which, with care, could be extended. However, Penfold had other plans as well.

In conjunction with other Clacton businessmen, Penfold had seen opportunities for amalgamation and further expansion in a different direction. By July 1897, Horace Spence, the secretary and manager of *Belle* Steamers, had been appointed a director of the reconstituted Walton-on-the-Naze Pier Company. With the new capital available this Company had set about a major extension of the pier and an improvement to the Clifton Hotel. By September 1897 the *Woolwich Belle* had already paid a courtesy visit to the town and had been well received. An amalgamation of *Belle* Steamers with this and other local companies would give both capital and expertise, that could be put to use further afield. It was too good an opportunity to be missed and as a major shareholder Penfold pressed for the winding up of *Belle* Steamers Ltd. so that a merger could take place. He got his way and on December 22nd 1897 *Belle* Steamers was voluntarily wound up. On January 7th 1898 The Coast Development Company was formed to take over the assets of five companies, namely:

> The Clacton-on-Sea Pier Company
> The Clacton-on-Sea General land, Building & Investment Co. Ltd. (1887)
> The Clacton-on-Sea Hall and Library Company
> The Belle Steamers Ltd., (1896)
> Walton-on-the-Naze Pier and Hotel Company (1866)

Of these only the Clacton-on-Sea Pier Company was not put into liquidation. The principal subscribers were:

A. Penfold, J.P., L.C.C.	Wine Merchant; Woolwich (Chairman)
G. W. Mitchell	Butcher
T. S. Cave	Engineer
C. Fleetwood-Pritchard	Barrister
J. G. White, J.P., L.C.C.	Brushmaker; (Deputy Chairman)
J. Topp	Silversmith
H. R. Spence	Manager of Steamboats

50

The Coast Development Company's Nominal Capital of £500,000 was divided into 40,000 preferential shares at five pounds each, and 60,000 ordinary shares again at five pounds each. On 1st February 1898 the new concern was duly registered as a limited company.

On April 7th 1898 yet another paddle steamer was launched by Denny Brothers. This was the Coast Development Company's penultimate vessel, named *Yarmouth Belle*. She had been ordered by *Belle* Steamers Ltd., on November 6th 1897 as a copy of *Walton Belle* and although she was slightly longer, she was equipped with the same triple expansion engines and internal fittings. After trials that showed her to be slightly slower than her sister, *Yarmouth Belle* left the Clyde on May 20th 1898 for the Thames. On her arrival she joined *Walton Belle* on the long service to Great Yarmouth where the availability of two vessels allowed the Coast Development Company far more flexibility in its operations.

Because of its size, the large *London Belle* still maintained the regular morning service to Southend and Clacton. But, as there was usually enough demand to warrant the use of two steamers on this morning service, it was decided to use either *Yarmouth Belle* or *Walton Belle* as a second vessel on this, the oldest and yet still the most popular, of their routes. Then, rather than exchange Yarmouth-bound passengers at Clacton, this second paddle steamer would continue on its way up the coast to arrive in the River Yare at about 6.30 p.m. Her sister vessel would have gone the opposite way from Great Yarmouth, arriving in London at about 9.30 p.m. This new shuttle service allowed *Clacton Belle* to be available for further excursion work and would explain how *Walton Belle*, having left Great Yarmouth at 9.30 a.m., could collide with a sailing barge named *Ada* near Wapping, later that evening. Fortunately, there was no loss of life in this incident although the barge, laden with bricks, sank after being towed to a nearby wharf. This change in the service did not affect the Great Yarmouth ''excursionist's sea trip'', to Clacton as the two ships were so time-tabled that passengers could still have time ashore.

Indeed, from July 25th 1898 excursionists were given the opportunity to visit a new destination, Walton-on-the-Naze. As previously mentioned, the pier was being improved at the time that it was taken over by the Coast Development Company and now, newly extended to a length of 2,610 feet, it reached out into deep water at all states of the tide. Added to this, the pier head had been significantly improved to allow two vessels to berth at any one time. From the Company's point of view, Walton now provided much better facilities than Clacton and, not surprisingly, it became the terminus for the London boat and therefore a more important stop for the East Coast paddle steamers than Clacton.

The developments at Walton-on-the-Naze did not really affect the General Steam Navigation Company as, even had they wished to call at the pier, landing rights would almost certainly have been denied them. As owners of the pier, the Coast Development Company jealously defended their virtual monopoly along the Essex coast. The only port to see 'Classical Birds' other than Great Yarmouth was Harwich, the Ha'penny Pier being frequently visited by General Steam Navigation's excursion vessels.

The new paddle steamer *Eagle* joined the General Steam navigation fleet during the summer of 1898. At two-hundred and sixty-five feet, *Eagle* was of a size between that of *London Belle* and *Southend Belle* and at first glance she resembled the *Belle* Steamers. Her promenade deck was carried forward to the mast but,

The General Steam Navigation Company's paddle steamer Eagle. *This photograph was probably taken at Deptford shortly before the start of the summer season.*

The only known photograph of Abel Penfold. It was through his drive and initiative that Belle *Steamers developed. Described as a ''...calm, clear headed man of business'', he was sorely missed by the Coast Development Company after his sudden death in February 1900.*

unlike the *Belle* Steamers, this deck projected slightly beyond it. Also, the fore saloon extended the full width of the ship and the paddle boxes were etched with a diamond pattern, reminicent of the 'Classical Birds'. All of these features were completely out of keeping with the established Denny pattern. With this modern and attractive vessel operating to Kent, the General Steam Navigation Company were in a much stronger position to compete with their rivals. *Eagle*'s appearance also allowed the Company to dismantle the old *Hoboken*. This vessel had been a favourite with the Great Yarmouth public for over a decade and in its way had probably done more to promote that service than any other paddle steamer. As it was, *Hoboken* passed into history without even a mention in the newspapers of the day.

With the demise of *Hoboken*, the General Steam Navigation Company's long East Coast service was left solely to their "Classical Birds". Although the direct nature of their route maintained their popularity, they presented no real competition to the "*Belles*" and the newly advertised stop at Southend did little more than delay them even further. Usually the *Belle* Steamer passed the General Steam Navigation vessel in the lower reaches of the Thames and despite the stops, usually arrived in Great Yarmouth first. By the close of the 1898 summer season, the Coast Development Company dominated the East Coast services. Never before had they experienced such a position of strength. The dominance of the *Belle Steamers* and the influx of capital resulting from the reorganisation prompted the Coast Development Company to expand during 1899. Previously, during August 1898, they had purchased Town Farm Estate at Southwold on the Suffolk coast.

Southwold was a small and rather exclusive holiday resort just south of Lowestoft which had been serviced by a narrow gauge railway since 1879. It was a regular port of call for excursion steamers from Lowestoft and Great Yarmouth but, because of the poor nature of its harbour, passengers had to be rowed ashore in small boats, weather permitting. The Coast Development Company saw possibilities for development and acted swiftly, but also, in their usual thorough manner. They constructed a road, Pier Avenue, from the railway station to the sea, and by July 1899 had laid the foundations of a large hotel on the sea front not far from Pier Avenue. The plans for this "commodious and elegant establishment", which was to be known as the Grand Hotel, had previously been exhibited in the Royal Academy London, where they had gained some acclaim. Working closely with the Town Council, the Coast Development Company divided the remaining land up into a hundred and twenty-three building plots which were then auctioned on August 19th 1899. At the pre-sale dinner in the town, Abel Penfold said that his Company were endeavouring to "advance the welfare of Southwold" and he foresaw that within the next few years "Southwold would be one of the most prosperous and frequented places on the East Coast of England". His Deputy, James White, then announced that a new pier, expected to cost nine thousand pounds, was soon to be built at the eastern end of Pier Avenue and that the wooden structure would be ready by the following summer. He further stated that the new paddle steamer then being constructed by Denny's at Dumbarton was to be named after the town, *Southwold Belle*. This news was greeted with great applause by those assembled.

While these developments were taking place at Southwold, the *Belle* Steamers sailed past the town without stopping. Their advertised services were much as they had been in the previous year with the Great Yarmouth service starting on June 4th, a month before that of the General Steam Navigation Company. Initially, either *Walton Belle* or *Yarmouth Belle* was based in Great Yarmouth, running each day to Walton-on-the-Naze and returning the same evening. But by August, the two vessels were running direct so that passengers did not have to change. However, the summer of 1899 did not pass as smoothly as previous summers for *Belle* Steamers. Contrary to popular belief, some of the more popular services did operate on Fridays. One of these was London to Clacton, and on the first trip of the season *Clacton Belle* was lost for the night in dense fog off the treacherous Essex coast south of Clacton. Much to the relief of passengers and crew the fog cleared in the morning and showed her to be off Southend where she berthed some fifteen hours late! During August the weather deteriorated and the *Belle* Steamer often failed to arrive in Great Yarmouth until late in the evening. The only consolation was that the General Steam Navigation were faring even worse; in one case *Laverock* and a complement of very sick passengers did not arrive until midnight. Nevertheless, despite the rough seas, the Bank Holiday demand required five vessels on the Saturday — the two *Belle* Steamers plus *Laverock*, *Halcyon* and *Philomel*, the atrocious weather conditions delaying *Philomel* to such an extent that she did not arrive until 2.00 a.m.!

If the August weather was not bad enough, the same month found three 'Belle' captains in court. Concern had been expressed by Margate Town Council as early as August 1893 that vessels using the "jetty" were overloaded and that no adequate check was made as to the number of passengers carried. Without doubt the regulations laid down by the Board of Trade were being blatantly flouted by all the large fleet operators. However, in August 1899 the Board of Trade pounced at Margate. Accurate checks were made on the number of passengers being carried by the paddle steamers and the captains of those vessels found to be overloaded were summonsed. Captain Andrews of the *Southend Belle* and two other captains, those of the *London Belle* and *Clacton Belle*, were fined a total of ninety-eight pounds. The Coast Development Company may have found solace in the fact that their fines were relatively small! Captain Holland on the *Royal Sovereign* was caught three times and fined forty-five pounds, plus two shillings and sixpence for each excess passenger! The aggregate number was so great that the total fine amounted to a staggering two-hundred and four pounds! New Palace Steamers must have been far from happy on that Bank Holiday as *Koh-i-Noor* was also caught and incurred fines totalling fifty pounds. Initially, more care was probably taken as regarding numbers but so great was demand that I am sure the regulations were soon again ignored. Certainly there were further court cases the following year, 1900, including one against Captain Mills of the *London Belle* who was fined just over twenty-eight pounds for having one hundred and forty-five excess passengers at Clacton.

However, the 1899 season ended happily for *Belle* Steamers with the presentation of the Royal Humane Society's award to Mr. Walter Huntingford, a seaman on the *London Belle*. In early August, during a rush to board the London boat at Clacton, a Mrs. Gates had lost her footing and fallen between the pier and the steamer. On hearing a cry Captain Mills had stopped the engines but to the horror of those witnessing the incident, Mrs. Gates was sucked under the vessel. Huntingford saw this happen and immediately dived in. Somehow he managed to extract the rather bruised lady from under the paddle box and bring her to safety. If it hadn't been for his quick thinking and the prompt action of Captain Mills in stopping the engines, Mrs. Gates would surely have been killed. As it was, both participants in this drama were able to find changes of clothing and continue with their journeys.

Unfortunately, the new century began badly for the Coast Development Company as on February 5th, 1900 its chairman, Abel Penfold, died aged sixty-seven. Quite apart from his being the driving force behind *Belle* Steamers, Penfold could also be described as one of the founding fathers of Clacton-on-Sea. Through the Woolwich Steam Packet Company he had supported Peter Schuyler Bruff in his early speculative venture and then later, through the various companies he was associated with, he had actively played his part in making the town what it is today. A man of vision and insight, the Company was to miss him. By a strange twist of fate, Peter Schuyler Bruff died shortly afterwards on February 24th, 1900 aged eighty-seven. Although he had not been a Director of the *Belle* Steamers he had always recognised their importance in the carefully planned development of both Clacton and Walton. Today Bruff is remembered in the east window of Walton parish church while Penfold has a road named after him in Clacton.

The relationship between Clacton-on-Sea and the Coast Development Company had, up to 1900, been good and both had prospered. However, in that year the Company diverted their vessels to Walton-on-the-Naze before coming to Clacton. From the Company's viewpoint this was economically sensible as the improved pier at Walton had good facilities and had already become known as the "meeting place of the *Belle* Steamers". It was also considerably safer as this route would avoid vessels having to use the 'Spitway', a narrow, shallow stretch of water by which vessels passed over the Gunfleet Sands and in which they all too often ran aground. I have lost count of the times I have read of *Belle* Steamers becoming stuck for several hours at a time. One can imagine the annoyance expressed on one occasion when the *London Belle* became hoplessly stuck on a falling tide only to be passed by the smaller *Yarmouth Belle* which sailed through with impunity. It was not unknown for passengers to be landed at Clacton by means of the ship's lifeboats! Under such circumstances a change of route seemed eminently sensible. However, this view was not shared by those in Clacton and a group of local businessmen embarked on a campaign to change the decision. It was suggested to the Urban District Council that they should buy Clacton Pier by compulsory purchase and then to re-open it to vessels of rival companies. If this was not possible then the Council should build a second pier. By stopping first at Walton it was felt that many of the London passengers would not bother to go on to Clacton. Obviously local traders felt that Walton would benefit at their expense and naturally feelings ran high.

Also, at Southwold work was not going smoothly. There, the good relationships between the Coast Development Company and the Town Council had deteriorated and the work on the gardens that stretched down towards the pier had stopped some two-hundred yards short. A lake had formed in the intervening space and the Council had refused to fill it up saying that it was nothing to do with them. The press were very scathing calling the Council "short-sighted" and "blind to their own interests". The Council procrastinated until threatened with a writ, whereupon they accepted liability and the 'pond' was filled in. This incident somewhat soured relationships.

Moreover, although *Southwold Belle* had almost been completed, she was not able to leave the Clyde until June 14th and so could not begin the East Coast summer service. This duty was left as usual to *Walton Belle*, which arrived in Great Yarmouth via Clacton, Walton and Southwold piers on June 2nd. Southwoldians had to wait until July 7th before *Southwold Belle* made its inaugural visit to their pier.

Southwold Belle's entry into service, however, brought to a close that period of growth that had begun in 1887. The years that led up to the outbreak of the Great War were destined to be very different.

THE "SOUTHWOLD BELLE."

SEA TRIPS.

To SOUTHWOLD, FELIXSTOWE, and WALTON-ON-THE-NAZE *(daily)*, by Belle Steamers, leaving Claremont Pier at 10 a.m., returning from Walton at 3 p.m., Felixstowe 3.30 p.m., Southwold 5.30 p.m. Saloon Return Fares, 2/-, 4/-, and 4/6.

This early view of Southwold Belle *was probably taken in the Thames estuary. The photograph was used to illustrate the 1907 Guide to Lowestoft.*

"Any more for the Belle?" .... What was a trip like? 3

With the commissioning of the final *Belle* Steamer, the *Southwold Belle*, it seems an appropriate time to pause and turn the attention to just what it was like to travel the North Sea on a paddle steamer. Few people today can remember such trips and so the information we have is gleaned from fading memories and what was written at the time. Postcards are particularly illuminating as they were often sold on the ships and became increasingly popular after 1900. Like other Companies, *Belle* Steamers had a set of cards especially printed for them and a selection has been used in illustrating this book. Quite naturally, many postcards just tell of a safe arrival but occasionally they graphically recount incidents that occurred, telling of excitement, boredom and often, the relief at arriving! Today these postcards themselves have travelled far and are found in shops throughout the British Isles.

In 1897, when the *Belle* Steamers extended their services to Great Yarmouth, a return journey to London was taken by a Mr. J. Hinde. Hinde lived in Lowestoft and may have been the son of a newspaper reporter. If so, he probably had reasonably easy access to the local press, which accounts for his having had published a long letter in which he recounted his "nautical" experiences. It is conceivable that his letter was sponsored but this is pure conjecture, and the letter remains a very detailed description of a journey taken over ninety years ago. For this reason I have reproduced it, virtually unaltered, as published at the time.

'Sir,

Given a July day with a cloudless sky, a pleasant breeze and a fine craft for a sea trip, the result ought to be an enjoyable time, provided, of course, that one is a good sailor.

The journey is divided into two sections. The first part is by steamer from Yarmouth to Clacton-on-Sea, spend about two hours ashore and then go on to London by another steamer, the one to Yarmouth returning thither after staying about half an hour at Clacton. The trip from Yarmouth is made in the company's newest and smartest craft, the *Walton Belle*. The title of *Yarmouth Belle* had already been appropriated by one of the Broadland excursion steamers. The *Walton Belle* is a Clyde built boat, having been constructed by the well known firm of Denny, of Dumbarton, who make a speciality of light draught paddle steamers of this class. She is 239 ft by 26 ft, with a gross tonnage of 464. All the strict regulations of the Board of Trade as to life-saving apparatus on board have been fully carried out, and everything in man's power seems to have been done to prevent accident. For the River Thames trips only she is licensed to carry 1087 passengers, for crossing the estuary of the Thames from Clacton to Herne Bay 692, whilst for the sea voyage to Great Yarmouth the number is restricted to 612. There are separate decks and saloons for first and second class passengers. The saloon is upholstered in blue frieze velvet, with blue and gold tapestry curtains and lighted when required, by electricity. Smokeless coal is burnt, and Messrs Denny's patent is used for arresting the sparks, and dust thrown out by the forced draught. This special boon can be most thankfully appreciated by those who know what it is to be smothered by smoke from a steamer's funnel. The engines are of the triple expansion type, and the comparative steadiness and absence of vibration (and consequently of a cause of feeling queer) all tend to enhance the pleasure of the trip.

Leaving Lowestoft by the 8.30 a.m. direct Yarmouth (and Broadland steamer) train, there is more than enough time to secure a good position on the upper deck of the *Walton Belle* before it starts from near Yarmouth Town Hall at 9.30. This is done very punctually, and the journey down the haven is made as quickly as consistent with safety in the comparatively narrow channel. The sharp bend near the mouth is successfully taken and the North Sea reached. Passing the ivy covered ruins of Corton Church and "The Clyffe", Lowestoft High Light is abreast of us about 10.20., and signals are soon exchanged with those on shore. Staying off the South Pier for a few moments to take aboard those who prefer to be put on board at Lowestoft from small boats, "full steam ahead" is soon resumed, Covehithe Ness rounded, and Southwold church and lighthouse sighted. Soon the ruins of some of East Anglia's ancient capital, Dunwich, are noticed, and also Thorpe Ness and Sizewell village. Aldeburgh is quickly passed, and the quaint old Elizabethen Moot Hall seen standing close to the beach, and on the cliff the tower of Aldeburgh church reminding us of Suffolk's chief poet, George Crabbe. Orford Ness lighthouse lies straight ahead and our steamer steers close to the point. The surf on the beach is plainly visible as we enter Hollesley Bay. To the seaward is the Shipwash light-ship, whilst on the shore the principal object is the massive Norman keep of Orford Castle. Felixstowe is the next place noticed, and the numerous bathing and family tents on the beach indicate the presence of many visitors. Landguard Fort with its usual camp and tents, appears just before the entrance to Harwich Harbour. The Parish church of the old Essex port is noticed, and also the masts of the craft in the harbour and alongside Parkestone Quay. The Naze at Walton is soon reached, and this town, which has somewhat declined of late since the rise of Clacton, shows some signs of going forward. A new suburb is springing up at Frinton-on-Sea. The "Grand" at Clacton is the first object we catch sight of in that town, and after making for the Pier Head, the *Walton Belle* is soon safely moored alongside and her passengers landed. A word of praise is due to the Clacton Pier Company and the *Belle* Company for having arranged for the latter's passengers to land, go off, and then come on to the pier again to board the steamer without making the irritating landing and embarking charges so beloved of many pier companies on the South Coast. Those who are returning to Yarmouth have about half to three quarters of an hour at Clacton, whilst London passengers have two hours. This latter just gives time to get some idea of the town. The Pier is a fair-sized one, with a large pavilion at its head. This is used for popular concerts and the like twice a day during the season. Its position is similar to that at Southend, at the bottom of the principal street. Clacton itself is flat, as is the surrounding country. The cliffs seem familiar to those who know those beyond Corton. The beach is well patronised, and of a sandy nature. The town appears to be increasing, and plots of land for sale are plentiful. It is a very modern place, and has only had a railway (the G. E. R.) for about 15 years.

Leaving Clacton for London at 4 p.m. in the *London Belle* (a larger boat than the *Walton Belle*), the first part of the course is straight out to sea, over a sandbank, past a buoy (the motion of the water causing the clapper to strike the bell) to the "Swin Middle" light-vessel, and then away past the Maplin Lighthouse, built on screw red iron piles and lighted by gas, to the westward of the dangerous Maplin Sands. Near a gas lit buoy, the Edinburgh and London passenger steamer, *Iona* is passed. This is where she caught fire one Sunday evening two years ago. Passing Foulness Island, and observing the numerous buoys and beacons which mark the treacherous sands and wrecks of vessels that have gone to pieces on them, and seeing the "Mouse" light vessel and Shoeburyness, Southend Pier is reached at about 6 p.m. Here some passengers are both landed and embarked. The longest pier in Great Britain is apparently not long enough, for it is being lengthened again, and is now about 1 mile and a half long. From here the famed "Nore" light vessel is seen. 1797 and the mutiny at the Nore! 1897 and the review at Spithead! Two most important epochs in the history of our Royal Navy. Looking across the estuary to the south, the coast of Kent can be seen, including the dockyard at Sheerness, the mouth of the Medway and a long stretch of hilly ground which reaches from Herne Bay to Margate.

The Pier, Clacton on Sea.

Clacton beach early this century. Although beach fashions have changed over the years, the pier still remains a great attraction. It was reopened to steamer traffic in 1988 but sadly, the London Belle *seen here leaving for Southend will never return.*

Usually, the distinctive funnel of the large London Belle *was only to be seen at Great Yarmouth on busy weekends. The largest vessel in the* Belle *fleet was more profitably used on services to Clacton and Margate.*

Steaming up the Thames, Leigh is on the right (Essex) side. A little further up the ruins of Hadleigh Castle are seen near to the farm colony of "General" Booth. Passing another red-pile lighthouse on Chapman Head, we move up the sea reach towards Tilbury. At Gravesend those who prefer to finish their journey to town by rail can land. Passengers for Victoria and other London, Chatham and Dover Company's stations continue their journey through Rosherville, Bromley, Beckenham, and Herne Hill. Those for the Great Eastern or London, Tilbury and Southend Companys' stations are also landed here and ferried across to Tilbury, whence they travel to Liverpool Street or Fenchurch Street. Victoria Station is reached at about 8.30 p.m. after an hour's ride through the pretty Kentish scenery and hop grounds. If the journey is finished by steamer, London Bridge is reached at about 9.30 p.m.

Returning the next morning, London Bridge is left punctually to time, 9.30, and in rapid succession came Billingsgate market, the Custom House and the historic Tower of London. Passing under the new Tower Bridge, the bascules of which have to be raised for the *London Belle*, St. Katharine's and the London Docks are seen. Before long Wapping, Rotherhithe, Shadwell, Deptford and the Isle of Dogs are left behind. The first stop is made at Greenwich, where are noticed the far-famed Hospital and Observatory. On past Blackwall, seeing Messrs. Maconochie's new works, to Canning Town and Woolwich, with its Royal Dockyard and arsenal. Beckton with it huge gasworks and sewage outfall are next to be passed. Here it is estimated that ten-million cubic feet of sewage are precipitated into the river each day. This great system of drainage for the mighty metropolis was designed by Sir John Bazalgette, whose connection with another outlet not quite so large may be remembered by some readers of the *Lowestoft Journal*. After Belvedere there appears the chalk pit of Purfleet where are the Government powder stores. Off Greenhithe lies the *Worcester*, a training ship for the merchant marine and the *Chichester* and *Arethusa* training ships for the destitute boys out of the London streets. Then, a little further on, off the Essex shore lay two more training vessels, the *Exmouth* and the *Shaftesbury*. The latter, is managed by the School Board for London and recently figured in the public press in connection with mismanagement. After Northfleet with its chalk cliffs and cement works we pass Rosherville. At nearby Gravesend passengers join us who have left Victoria or Fenchurch Street by train at the same time that we left London Bridge. Soon after leaving we pass the fine P. & O. vessel *India* from which survivors from the ill-fated *Aden* had been landed a few days before. Another P. & O. vessel, the *Scotia* is also passed. By a somewhat singular coincidence, she had been named after the island on which the *Aden* had been wrecked last month. Southend is reached at about mid-day and soon we are on course for Clacton-on-Sea. This course is a little different from that which we came by. The pier is reached at about 2.30, and changing to the *Walton Belle* we are soon again *en route* to Yarmouth. The *Woolwich Belle* is waiting for any passengers who may wish to go to Felixstowe, Harwich or Ipswich.

Leaving Clacton at 2.45, we pass Walton, Dovercourt and beyond it Landguard Fort. At 4 p.m. we are abreast of Bawdsey Ferry and Haven where a large hotel is being built. Orford Ness lighthouse appears as a white speck on the horizon and slowly grows as we approach. The very lonely situation of this lighthouse is again impressed upon our minds, and we wonder if the visitors' book commenced in 1857 is yet filled up. There was plenty of space left when it was visited (after a dreary walk across the Sahara of shingle) last August. From Orford Ness to Covehithe Ness was the roughest part of the whole trip. The choppy seas washed over the bow of the *Walton Belle* and some of her passengers who enjoy the sensation were reminded that to others it was anything but a pleasure. Aldeburgh and Southwold are soon left behind and Lowestoft comes in sight. Leaving some passengers in the shore boat, Yarmouth is reached at about 7 p.m. The *Walton Belle* is turned round in the bend at the harbour mouth, and proceeds up the Haven stern foremost, so as to be ready for her start on the next voyage. Bidding Captain Prior farewell, with a promise to report him and his careful seamanship, the day is finished with a trip to the Beach Gardens Jetty where a steamer of a rival line was seen coming in. This vessel had started before us and had been passed near Gravesend.

To anyone who desires a good sea blow, and who can spare but one day, there can be no better way of getting it than to go to Clacton and back, as described above. If a longer journey can be made the trip to London can be highly recommended. Return tickets can be had at cheap rates and are available until the end of the season.

On the voyage occur many incidents which tend to relieve any feeling of monotony or tediousness. Amongst the passengers is one of the Argyll and Sutherland Highlanders in uniform. Pockets not being plentiful in the kilt, the Highlander had utilised the turn-down portion of his sock wherein to carry his boat ticket. this novel ticket holder caused some little amusement to those who noticed it. On the down trip on the *London Belle*, Captain Mills sent one of the stewards of the boat all over it to give a warning: ''Ladies, look after your purses!'' There was evidently a London thief on board, as a loss had been reported to the Captain. Anyone who can give particulars of the places passed is eagerly sought after, and if missing for a little while is looked for and told he is wanted to tell some passengers where they are. Many curious remarks are heard, and those who know the least about ships and the coast are the most assertive as to what they are talking about.

An official guide for the whole route, London to Ymouth, is published. This appears to be accurate as far as the Harwich — Ipswich section. Beyond this, however, strangers to the locality must be warned against the particulars it contains as there are glaring errors. It is difficult for a writer to describe a locality with which he is unfamiliar and a little local help would have surely avoided such obvious mistakes.

Yours faithfully,
A. H. Hinde.

I think it is safe to suggest that the weather was kind to Mr. Hinde, but this was not always so. In 1902 another Lowestoft observer confessed that ''curiosity impelled me to visit the new Claremont Pier to see what manner of braves they were who had come from London in the teeth of a stinging norther. There were a fair number aboard suggesting that steamer passengers were not put off by a North Sea gale. Some thirty or forty passengers disembarked and as I watched their arrival I concluded that it was probably warmer afloat than ashore''. I'm not sure how he reached this conclusion, but it prompted him to board the *Walton Belle* for the rest of the journey to Great Yarmouth and he continues, ''once the steamer had cast off I was sadly disillusioned. The northerly wind whistled through the rigging and the spray from the inky black waves was like the lashing of whips. There was a large crowd to watch our arrival at Gorleston and although shivering, we were rather proud of the attention bestowed. And, all this for one shilling! You cannot expect more than a seven mile sea trip and throngs to greet you for less than twelve pennies''.

''Feeding the fishes'' was also a popular pastime. The short sharp waves created by the shallow North Sea are common throughout the year and today we can only imagine the conditions that prevailed aboard these crowded steamers. None of the vessels had the luxury of stabilisers, and the toilets were by the standards of today's ferries, very rudimentary. If you were lucky you might have had a chamber pot, but usually the sides of the vessel provided the only relief. A few years ago a 'pot' bearing the insignia of the General Steam Navigation Company was trawled up off Aldeburgh. It had lost its handle and one can only speculate as to the drama it had witnessed.

Illness or injuries at sea could prove to be very serious. Today's facilities were not available to steamer captains and the vessels carried no doctors. Injuries, whether minor or serious were treated by members of the ship's crew while the vessel continued on its course. One gentleman who became seriously ill was merely comforted until the *Hoboken* arrived at Great Yarmouth. No attempt was made to put him ashore at Lowestoft where a modern (1892) hospital was located. Once in port the unfortunate gentleman was rushed to hospital where he died shortly afterwards.

Running between June and October the vessels had the best of the weather and seldom failed to sail. Occasionally they were caught out during the passage which is not really surprising as contemporary weather forecasts lacked any accurate prediction. In one of the more serious incidents *Seine* ran into a gale soon after leaving the Thames. She battled up the coast until off Southwold the wind veered to the North East and her captain decided that for the safety of his passengers he would seek shelter. Unable to make Lowestoft he turned and ran with the wind towards Felixstowe where with difficulty he rounded Landguard Fort to lay up off Harwich. We are not told what happened to the passengers, only that the vessel resumed her journey the next day. A similar gale was encountered by *Glen Rosa* in 1893 when soon after leaving Great Yarmouth weather conditions forced a return to port. In this case passengers were sent to their various destinations by rail, at the expense of the Victoria Steamboat Association.

Storms and *mal de mer* may have been the concern of the passengers but it was fog that worried crews. These vessels had no radar, radios, or satellite navigation systems, to guide them. Instead, their captains relied heavily on visual contacts. Buoys, lighthouses, and the then more numerous lightships, all gave accurate positions, added to which, by sailing close inshore the captain provided his passengers with scenic views and himself with a continual confirmation of his position! However, when fog descended the North Sea became very inhospitable. Navigation then relied on the compass and the keen ears of the crew. The busy Thames estuary was navigated through a maze of channels and one mistake could and often did mean hours of delay waiting for the next tide. Further north, off Southwold and Lowestoft shifting sandbanks could spell disaster. At pier heads the pier-masters often waited many hours for overdue vessels crowded with passengers. In London and Great Yarmouth large crowds anxiously awaited the arrival of overdue steamers late into the night. Without radios, alarm and anxiety spread quickly amongst those waiting. When in 1894 *La Marguerite* was a few hours late in returning from France, talk of disaster abounded, causing much distress amongst waiting relatives. The welcome sight of navigation lights coming up the river always caused a ripple of relief amongst those ashore.

Although the various companies always advertised "weather and circumstances permitting" it was usually "circumstances" that delayed the vessel's departure or even arrival. Breakdowns were not uncommon and happened to vessels of all the different companies at one time or another. Sometimes problems developed during a journey but the vessel was able to proceed without the passengers realising that anything was amiss. In London or Great Yarmouth men would work through the night to get the ship ready for the following day. But, if the problem were more serious, the ship would be withdrawn until repaired. In these cases schedules were rearranged or a replacement vessel acquired. Occasionally, as at Great Yarmouth where no alternative vessel could be found, we find that the following days sailing was cancelled, passengers being left to find their way home by other means. Occasionally vessels broke down completely whilst at sea. Today, this would be regarded with alarm, but a century ago it was regarded as just one of those irritating problems associated with steamer travel. On most occasions the engineers quickly repaired the faults and the engines were started; however, sometimes they were not. When this happened the attitudes shown by both passengers and crew were rather surprising as the following incident involving *Glen Rosa* reveals.

On August 8th 1893, *Glen Rosa* was making her regular voyage from Harwich to Great Yarmouth when at 6.45 p.m. an engineer reported that something was wrong with the port paddle wheel. Captain Reader ordered an examination and it was found that a bolt from one of the supporting rods to the paddle floats had sheered. The engines were stopped and the vessel brought to a halt close to the sandbanks off Covehithe Ness. This was not an ideal place to stop and after discussion with the engineers the vessel was moved at half speed to a safer anchorage. Unfortunately this only exacerbated the problem by disconnecting the rod and splitting the float. The two-hundred passengers were told that repairs would only take half an hour. Fortunately, the sea was calm and the passengers whiled away the time singing and dancing to a small band. Soon after starting on the repairs it was found that rust prevented the removal of the metal plates from the broken float and that the rod would have to be cut away. It was obviously going to be a much longer job than at first thought. The paddle tug *Rainbow* arrived from Lowestoft and offered to take *Glen Rosa* in tow. At first Captain Reader declined but then changed his mind and offered ten pounds for a tow to Great Yarmouth. *Rainbow*'s captain refused and asked for twenty-five pounds. The passengers continued dancing while the haggling continued. The two captains failed to agree terms and the *Rainbow* abandoned *Glen Rosa* to the night. Lowestoft beach yawls appeared and took off the ''few'' passengers who were eager to leave. Shortly after, the Great Yarmouth paddle tugs *Yare* and *Meteor* arrived. *Yare* came alongside and her captain went aboard *Glen Rosa* to ''talk terms''. An offer of fifteen pounds was made by Captain Reader but this was refused and fifty pounds was asked. Captain Reader stated that he thought that this amount was ''ridiculously large to ask under the circumstances''. By this time it was ten o'clock and the passengers were said to be ''getting tired''. They remonstrated with Captain Reader and urged him to agree terms but he declined to accede to to their demands and the *Yare* returned alone to Great Yarmouth. With *Meteor* standing by and the passengers settled in the crowded saloon, *Glen Rosa*'s engineers worked on until at about 11.15 p.m. she weighed anchor. A few spectators watched her arrival in Great Yarmouth at about 12.30 a.m.! Although some passengers were annoyed at being misinformed, public confidence was not shaken, in fact over two-hundred passengers sailed for Harwich the following morning.

Other breakdowns were more dramatic. On 20th August 1906, the paddle steamer *Laverock* was making her usual voyage to London when off Covehithe (again!) she came to a sudden halt. A main steampipe had ruptured resulting in the engines being starved of power. Repairs were quite impossible and all that could be done was to await assistance. Fortunately the fears of the passengers were soon allayed by the appearance of the *Belle* Steamer that had just left Lowestoft and *H. M. S. Argus*. *Laverock*'s captain decided that a tow was required and so the passengers were unexpectedly returned to Great Yarmouth by courtesy of the Royal Navy. No record is made as to whether a charge was levied! By a strange twist of fate a postscript to this story has since come to light. According to the local press *Laverock* had arrived at Great Yarmouth very late on the previous evening but no explanation was given. However, a hastily written postcard dated August 19th 1906 was recently found in Norwich. Its writer states that he had arrived in Great Yarmouth very late on the *Laverock* after breaking down three times during the journey from London! So it appears that the vessel broke down on consecutive days and one may speculate that the repairs of the 19th were just too temporary.

The bascules of Tower Bridge were opened to allow Belle Steamers *to sail through. Here* Clacton Belle *passes down river on her way to Greenwich and the coast.*

THE PIER, WALTON-ON-THE-NAZE.

Walton-on-the-Naze became an important stop for the Belle Steamers *after the pierhead had been improved. This photograph was taken between 1898 and 1900 and shows four vessels, including* London Belle, Southwold Belle, *and* Woolwich Belle. *At this date the shore end of the pier had not been completed and one of the pier's trams was being used as a waiting room.*

Passengers did not always experience the luxury of a tow. In some cases they were expected to transfer, complete with their baggage from one vessel to another whilst at sea. In August 1903, *Halcyon* became "incapacitated" soon after leaving the river Yare. With her steering gear broken danger signals were hoisted and the vessel brought up. The sea was rough and the passengers had an uncomfortable wait for assistance.

The *Southwold Belle* was the first vessel to arrive on the scene and her captain quickly offered to take aboard all those passengers bound for London. This was agreed and the two vessels manoeuvred alongside each other. The fixing of a gangway was made more difficult by the curiosity of passengers who had congregated to one side so as to watch the proceedings. The list created was considerable and it was only after repeated pleas from the captain to balance the boat that the transfer of the passengers and their baggage could begin. When this was complete *Southwold Belle* proceeded on her way with an "unusually heavy load". One wonders whether certain "conditions" stipulated by the Board of Trade were flouted?

The passengers of *Southwold Belle* would have also had the experience of passing under the raised bascules of Tower Bridge as they ended their journey. Tower Bridge, opened in 1894, needed to be raised for all the *Belle* and General Steam Navigation vessels. Passengers on the New Palace Steamers, *Koh-i-Noor* or *Royal Sovereign* would not have witnessed this. Instead, they might have been bemused to see their captain pull down a pair of goggles. Any giggling soon ceased as the reasons for this strange behaviour became obvious. At this point in the journey large steam winches began to retract the telescopic funnels. As the height of the funnels decreased, the amount of smoke swirling around the deck increased covering the unwary with sooty smuts. As New Palace Steamers still sailed from Old Swan Pier, the vessel then needed to be carefully positioned in the river so that she could slip through the central arch of London Bridge. There was more smoke and irritation as the vessel shot through to her moorings just beyond. What a way to end what may have already been a harrowing trip!

In mentioning the captain's goggles I have touched upon another important element of the journey, namely the crew. Few could have failed to be impressed by the gleaming pistons that were tended with such care by the hard-working engineers. Engineers who with oil cans in hand would delight children with the occasional upward squirt in their direction. Certainly these men were colourful characters who would so often relieve any feelings of monotony or tediousness. They were employed on a seasonal basis, spend ing the remaining months of the year in other vessels or as fishermen. Their cabins were situated in the bow of the ship and by all accounts were rather cramped — quite the opposite to the spacious accommodation provided for the clientele. Indeed, many crew members chose not to stay on board if they could possibly help it. In London they preferred to lodge near the river returning to the ship early in the morning to prepare for sea. In Great Yarmouth, summer accommodation was much more difficult to find and often the vessels provided the only opportunity of a bed. They might have been tough but by all accounts they had hearts of gold and the knowledge of how to make an extra penny or two! They would sell 'hat guards' to those not wishing to lose their 'boaters' overboard on windy days. It was not unknown for them to promote sales by discreetly throwing overboard a few old hats and then point these out to unwary passengers. Some would also encourage the idea that it was lucky to toss pennies down the large ventilators that led cool air to the boiler room. The cash was collected in a bucket by the hard-working stokers far below and later shared out. These men were often mercenary, owing no allegiance to any one company. Although they would often sign on for the season it was not unknown for them to change companies during the summer. This was especially true if one resort held more 'attractions' than another!

The captains were different only in that they were employed all year or paid a retainer. It was their responsibility to see that the ship was well prepared for the summer season. They too were popular men, prepared to chat to passengers whenever they had the opportunity. Like the rest of the crew they were opportunists, moving from company to company in search of more prestigious commands and higher wages. However, by 1900 *Belle* Steamers employed a number of popular captains many of whom were to remain with them throughout the Edwardian period. Probably the most renowed was Captain Edward Mills, senior. I put 'senior' because one of his sons, also Edward commanded vessels in the *Belle* fleet, most notably *Woolwich Belle*. Another son, Thomas, also worked for a time as Chief Officer under his father on *Clacton Belle,* before becoming master of the *Walton Belle*. It was certainly a family concern! Edward (senior) was born in 1853 at Woolwich and had first gone to sea at the age of seven as a 'call boy' on the paddle steamer *Stork.* In 1864 he was employed aboard the paddle steamer *Queen of the Thames* which was regularly running to Ipswich, and in 1871 he had been the helmsman of the *Queen of the Orwell* at the time that she had first visited Bruff's new pier at Clacton. It was a pier the Mills always thought poorly sited. In 1881 he was appointed as master of the *Glen Rosa* by the newly formed Victoria Steamboat Association and he sailed this vessel between London, Clacton and Ipswich. This was in direct competition with the London, Woolwich and Clacton-on-Sea Steamboat Company's steamer *Clacton.* During 1889 he had been privileged to be chosen to command the paddle steamer *Duke of Edinburgh,* assigned to carry Edward, Prince of Wales to Gravesend, to, meet the Shah of Persia. Captain Mills then brought both back up the Thames to London, a task for which he was thanked by the Admiralty. In the following year, 1890, he left the Victoria Steamboat Association to join the London, Woolwich and Clacton-on-Sea Steamboat Company. As an experienced paddle steamer captain he was immediately given a prestigious command, the new *Clacton Belle.* This was a position he held until 1893 when he was appointed to command the *London Belle.* Even the *Dumbarton Herald* commented at the time on his great expertise in navigating on the crowded waters of the Thames. Edward (senior) stayed with the Company until November 1900 when he was appointed by Trinity House as a Thames Pilot. He worked in this capacity until his retirement in 1923. Living in Northfleet enabled him to visit Clacton regularly right up until his death at the age of 96 in July 1949.

These characters have now gone and the sea trips are a thing of the past. Technological progress has not always given us choice, for today there are few places where one can take a trip out to sea, let alone a coastal passage. A century ago life was more exacting, perhaps even exciting. Certainly going on holiday was more than an adventure! It is probably best to think of a paddle steamer journey in the way that Mr. Hinde concluded, ''for anyone who desires a good sea blow and who can spare but one day, there can be no better way of getting it''.

Mounting Problems **4**

The period from 1900 until the outbreak of the Great War in 1914 was one of apparent stability. The cut-throat competition that had marked the period from 1887 had gone. Although vessels were bought and sold, the surviving steamship companies appeared settled and their routes well established. The competition between steamship operators had been replaced by increased competition from the railway companies. This competition was far more insidious as it threatened the very existence of many paddle steamer routes and was to lead to an increased emphasis being placed on the shorter excursion trade as a means of maintaining financial viability. This period beginning in 1900 was one in which new problems were revealed, problems that would eventually prove insurmountable.

The Edwardian decade has been called the ''heyday of the paddle steamer'' and it represents an overall picture of crowded vessels and booming holiday resorts. Although this view is to a large extent true, it can also be deceptive as the period has been well recorded pictorially. Paddle steamers make picturesque subjects and are frequently found on contemporary postcards. Unfortunately, these photographs were quite naturally taken on bright summer days and do not record the rough days on which — as we know from newspaper reports — the vessels arrived late and virtually empty. On those days an increasingly discerning public came to the East Coast resorts by train, preferring a four hour journey to Great Yarmouth in the new comfort of a third class carriage to at least nine hours in the open well deck of a steamer for almost the same price. Ironically the very problem faced by the paddle steamer operators was that of stability. After the numerous developments in design found during the previous decades, the first ten years of the new century saw little change in East Coast paddle steamers. This was not the case with the railway companies whose new and attractive facilities were continually being developed. Passenger comfort and train speeds had increased while safety standards had risen to such an extent that in 1901 the railway companies could boast that not one passenger life was lost through their fault. It has been estimated that ninety-five per cent of rail passengers travelled third class paying about a half-penny per mile, this being half its former level! These were the very passengers that paddle steamer operators had to coax onto their vessels! Although the comfort and high standards found in the paddle steamers were maintained the social changes and technological developments that marked the Edwardian period either passed by or were ignored by most paddle steamer companies.

Southwold Belle, the last and probably the finest vessel to have been owned by the Coast Development Company, is best described as being an improved version of the earlier *Yarmouth Belle*. She had been ordered by the Coast Development

Company in April 1899 soon after their reorganisation and had been launched by Denny Brothers at Dumbarton on May 3rd 1900. She had been contracted to reach a speed of sixteen and a half knots but, on trials between the Cloch and Cumbrae lighthouses, she managed 17.19 knots using fifteen feet eight inch diameter wheels. It is interesting, that on a similar trial using fifteen foot paddle wheels she made only 16.85 knots. Perhaps the most striking difference between *Southwold Belle* and her near sisters was that her fore-saloon extended over the full width of the vessel. She was the only *Belle* Steamer so built and in this respect she resembled the General Steam Navigation Company's paddle steamer *Eagle*. Another noticeable feature was that a small extension to the promenade deck reached almost to her mast. *Southwold Belle* was built some five feet longer than *Yarmouth Belle* so, in length, she was approaching the dimensions of *Southend Belle*. It seems extraordinary that the three final *Belle* Steamers were not built to the same specifications as all three vessels carried the same B.O.T. No. 3 certificate and were to be used on similar services, primarily that to Great Yarmouth. Had they been built to the same design, building costs would have been significantly reduced. As it was this 535 gross ton vessel cost the Coast Development Company £27,265 although, as with other vessels, she was probably mortgaged from her builders.

With *Southwold Belle* entering service, the *Belle* Steamer fleet was complete and the general pattern of the 1900 services followed that of the previous year. The controversial stop at Walton before Clacton raised its head again at a meeting of the Clacton Urban District Council in December 1900 when councillors stated that the cost of a proposed new pier would be prohibitive. It was agreed that overtures should be made to the Coast Developement Company to persuade them to reverse their unpopular decision in time for the 1901 season. Nevertheless, in that same week the *Clacton Graphic* published a popular picture of the pier with the caption, "This pier or a new one?".

In the new year a mortgage of thirteen thousand pounds was taken out by the Coast Development Company on Clacton Pier. Just why there was a need for this injection of capital is unclear. However, it may have been to help finance the building of a new pier at Lowestoft. The Company had never been happy with the transfer of passengers into small boats for landing, and had decided as early as 1900 to construct a pier on the south beach at the seaward end of Claremont Road. This structure was to be called the South Pier but as this name was already used for a pier adjacent to Lowestoft Harbour, the company settled on the name "Claremont Pier". Unlike their neighbours at Southwold, the Lowestoft Town Council were very enthusiastic and appreciative of the interest shown by the Coast Development Company and took a great interest in the project. But the building of the Claremont Pier progressed very slowly and the structure was not to be finished until the summer of 1903. Until that date steamers continued to transfer their passengers at sea and land them from small boats on the beach.

The service for 1901 began in late May with the London day boat again visiting Walton before Clacton. Soon, a full scale row developed and the *Clacton Graphic* led the assault on the Coast Development Company with a scathing attack on Horace Spence, the Company's General Manager. Throughout the season letters appear giving or seeking advice on the matter of "The Spitway". By late September a communication from the Trinity Brethren rejecting any idea of deepening the Channel and suggesting instead that the matter be left in the hands of nature. From Clacton's point of view there was little more that could be done

CLAREMONT PIER, LOWESTOFT.

An early view of Lowestoft's Claremont Pier, taken before the pier head was extended. The vessel is probably London Belle.

An early photograph of Southwold Pier and Walton Belle, *taken from the Grand Hotel. Although its construction removed the need for passengers to be rowed ashore, it did not generate the crowds seen in other resorts.*

and it seemed only to add insult to injury when the small *Woolwich Belle* ran aground in what had been hitherto the safe approach from Walton!

Apart from the continuing arguments over "The Spitway", the 1901 season was probably remembered by the Coast Development Company for one tragic incident. In September a jury returned a verdict of Accidental Death in an inquest into the death of John Bryant aged fifty-three. Bryant, accompanied by his wife and daughter, had boarded the *London Belle* for a trip to Clacton. Soon after leaving Tilbury, Bryant casually leant against the abaft port gangway rail. To the horror of his family the rail suddenly collapsed pitching the unfortunate Bryant into the river. He was immediately sucked under the stern of the vessel and disappeared. Later that day a barge found his body and took it up to London where a post mortem revealed multiple fractures to ribs, spine and skull. Death had probably been "instantaneous". Subsequent enquiries found that the gangway bolts were insecure and were the direct cause of the accident. Perhaps surprisingly, the court found that there was insufficient evidence to show where responsibility rested and the Coast Development Company escaped prosecution. Public attitudes have certainly changed in the intervening years. In my research for this book, the Bryant incident is the only fatal accident involving a passenger on a *Belle* Steamer which I have found.

Perhaps the Coast Development Company was also lucky not to have lost one of their vessels during the season. On July 6th 1901, while *Walton Belle* was off a particularly windswept and desolate part of the Suffolk coast near Sizewell, the vessel became incapacitated, and with over three hundred passengers aboard she slowly drifted towards the beach. Fortunately. the Great Yarmouth paddle tug *King Edward VII* had just completed the first part of its inaugural summer excursion trip to Southwold and was able to go to the aid of the stricken vessel. *King Edward VII* towed *Walton Belle* to Harwich where in the early hours of Sunday morning the passengers were disembarked, returning to London by rail. I have often speculated as to what happened to the Southwold "trippists" who had purchased return tickets and who must have wondered where *King Edward VII* had got to. Perhaps they returned home via the infamous Southwold Railway or by the new motor coach services.

The only development to benefit the Coast Development Company in 1901 was the opening of the Grand Hotel Southwold in time for the August Bank Holiday weekend. On that Saturday both *Southwold Belle* and *Yarmouth Belle* landed passengers at Southwold, the pier head being only a few hundred yards from the new hotel. Soon after the two steamers arrived in Great Yarmouth the *Southwold Belle* returned to London. However, only a few passengers took advantage of this unusual night trip.

The Coast Development Company hoped that 1902 would prove to be happier than the previous season and with the coronation due in June they, along with the whole country, looked forward to the festivities.

A large naval fleet assembled at Spithead during the second half of June for the Coronation Review. In order to accommodate the large number of visitors wishing to inspect the lines of warships, three of the *Belle* fleet were chartered by South Coast and Continental Steamers of Southampton. These were the *Walton Belle*, *Southwold Belle* and *Yarmouth Belle*, the most economic vessels in the fleet. It was intended to run the three vessels from Southampton on excursions around the fleet. As these three steamers maintained the Great Yarmouth service, adverts for that summer announced that there would be no vessels except *Woolwich Belle* running north of Walton between June 25th and July 1st. Unfortunately, on June 25th the press announced that the King had undergone an emergency appendectomy and that the coronation had been postponed. But the fleet had already assembled and, as the ships presented a considerable attraction, the charters were taken up and both *Southwold Belle* and *Walton Belle* were advertised as sailing from Royal Pier, Southampton on "trips to view the fleet". I have found no mention of *Yarmouth Belle* in the Solent or at Great Yarmouht so her where abouts are unknown during this period. Just prior to the coronation, Mr. Elliott, the refreshment contractor for *Belle* Steamers, had had a disagreement with a seating agency over accommodation on the *Walton Belle* during the proposed charters. In the resulting court case it was suggested that modified south coast excursions might be arranged. Certainly, the *Woolwich Belle*'s 'Coronation Trip' to the local lightships went ahead as planned. Captain Holland went to great lengths to give passengers the opportunity to put gifts aboard the various vessels. He felt that their crews suffered particular hardships in their lonely occupation.

1902 also saw the withdrawal of an old favourite from Thames waters. This was the *Lord of the Isles*, the vessel which had so impressed Londoners when she was first brought down from Scotland by the Victoria Steamboat Association. In later years, while under the control of P. W. Black's "Planet Steamers", she had been known as *Jupiter* and had been a regular visitor to Margate. *Jupiter* returned to the Clyde where she was rechristened *Lady of the Isles*. Unfortunately, by 1902 she was too old and lacking in the sophistication necessary for her to compete effectively with her Clyde rivals. It was not surprising that she was scrapped after only one season. Although *Jupiter*'s withdrawal from the Thames benefitted 'Belle Steamers' it was more keenly felt by the General Steam Navigation Company and New Palace Steamers who, between them, provided the main services from London to Kent.

Naturally, the withdrawal of one rival was regarded favourably by *Belle* Steamers and the following year 1903, they had further cause for celebrations in the opening of the new pier at Lowestoft. At 8 a.m. on May 30th, 1903 the pier was opened without ceremony by simply taking a penny from the first customer. By 6 p.m. when *Walton Belle* was timed to arrive, many thousands of people had passed through the turnstiles. Although the *Walton Belle* was three quarters of an hour late arriving, many hundreds had gathered to witness the event. Only thirty-three passengers disembarked but these included Horace Spence, the General Manager of *Belle* Steamers. A gun fired to mark the arrival and departure of the ship, brought many more people to the cliffs. It transpired that they thought the gun had signalled the launch of the lifeboat! The sucessful opening day concluded with a concert performed on a temporary stage erected about half way along the structure.

Although it was the first boat of the season, thirty-three passengers disembarking at Lowestoft does not seem very many. Indeed, throughout the season passenger numbers caused concern. The Coast Development Company — with its virtual monopoly along the Essex and Suffolk coasts to Great Yarmouth — were not seriously affected by this; however, it did concern the General Steam Navigation Company. They were also experiencing an increasing number of mechanical problems with their ageing 'Classical Birds'. New Palace Steamers were also forced to examine their services. Although *Royal Sovereign* and *Koh-i-Noor* were as popular as ever, the Company was losing money. The parent company, Fairfields, decided that the reason for this lay in the enormous running costs incurred by *La Marguerite*. Although often crowded, her services to Belgium and France were not really profitable. Moreover, she took passengers to Margate that could otherwise be accommodated on either of their other vessels. It was therefore announced that *La Marguerite* would be withdrawn at the close of the 1903 season. As Fairfields also controlled the Liverpool and North Wales Steamship Company, it was decided to transfer *La Marguerite* to their fleet. She was placed on the Liverpool, Llandudno and Menai Bridge service where there was an urgent need for a larger vessel. Over the years she proved to be a popular vessel and great sadness was expressed when in 1925 she was eventually withdrawn and scrapped. Her removal from the Thames served only to highlight the problem faced by all Thames operators, that of over-capacity. Avoiding these difficult problems, George Harvey, the Great Yarmouth representative of *Belle* Steamers, stated at a dinner marking the closure of the 1903 season, that from a commercial point of view the town was indebted to the steamships which, he felt, could do no more to increase their capacity.

The removal of *La Marguerite* resulted in a reorganisation of Thames services in 1904. Anxious to replace their continental routes with something more profitable, New Palace Steamers decided to extend their Kent services. In order to do this *Koh-i-Noor* was based at Tilbury from where she sailed each Monday, Wednesday and Thursday to Southend, Margate, Ramsgate, Deal and Dover. Being based at Tilbury enabled her on other days to do twice daily return trips to Margate. As in the case of *La Marguerite*, passengers reached Tilbury by special boat trains from St. Pancras or Fenchuch Street. *Koh-i-Noor* was to remain on this route right up until July 1914.

This move by New Palace Steamers did not affect the *Belle* Steamers who found enough custom for their usual service to Southend and the Kent resorts. The success of the pier at Lowestoft had led during the year to the building of a similar structure at Felixstowe. This, it was hoped, would remove the reliance on the Great Eastern Railway's Riverside Pier which the company had hitherto used. As far as the Coast Development Company was concerned, Riverside Pier suffered from a number of disadvantages, the most important being that the Coast Development Company were not the owners and were therefore beholden to the Great Eastern Railway for landing rights. As ship owners themselves, the railway company were obviously protective towards their own Orwell services and this had always inhibited *Woolwich Belle*'s services. Secondly, being situated at the mouth of the river meant that the pier was bypassed by the London to Great Yarmouth vessels. Passengers for Felixstowe had first to change at Walton to the *Woolwich Belle* and then find transport from Riverside pier to the town centre which was some distance away. A seafront pier, close to the resorts growing number of amenities would be far more satisfactory.

By 1904 the Coast Development Company had reversed its earlier decision to go to Walton before Clacton. Why they changed their minds is unclear as the 'Spitway' was no deeper and once more *London Belle* soon found herself aground! It seems extraordinary that the Company should have bowed to the Clacton pressure groups. The economic motives behind those in Clacton are all too obvious and such a forceful press campaign was quite in keeping with the town's dynamic spirit, although, quite what those in Walton thought about it is unclear. I can see no economic benefits for the Coast Development Company from this change and can only conclude that the change in attitude probably reflects the less forceful management that followed the death of Abel Penfold.

By the following year the Coast Development Company's financial situation was causing concern and at a meeting on March 8th 1905 a resolution was passed stating that the Company would be wound up prior to further reconstruction. Later that month this decision was confirmed and a new company was launched under the title of the Coast Development Corporation. On March 27th 1905 the new company was registered by Walter Young and Sons to take over the assets of the former Coast Development Company. Its objectives were to develop resources along the East Coast or elsewhere within the United Kingdom with particular attention to land, shops, public halls, libraries, piers and ships. Its directors were those of the old company:

T. S. Cave	Engineer	Woking
G. Riley	Engineer	Walton-on-Thames
H. R. Spence	Manager	Hampstead
J. G. White	Manager	London
J. M. Denny M.P.	Shipbuilder	Dumbarton
C. F. Pritchard	Barrister	Temple
G. W. Mitchell	Butcher	Woolwich

The most interesting name on this list is undoubtedly that of J. M. Denny of the shipbuilding family. Throughout the pre-war period Denny Brothers were represented on the Board of Directors. By doing this they matched their great Clyde rivals, Fairfields in having an interest in a shipping company. Also, they were able to keep an eye on their investments — the steamers still mortgaged to the Coast Development Corporation! This was a wise move on the part of Denny's as the Corporation could not sit back on its laurels. The financially buoyant General Steam Navigation Company were always a potential threat to the Corporation's virtual monopoly along the east coast.

In September 1905 the General Steam Navigation Company made a significant move by ordering a new excursion and cross channel steamer. It was a bold move as it showed that they still believed that, given the right vessels, a profit could be made from continental services. *La Marguerite* had been too costly to run while their own 'Classical Birds', though often running continental excursions, were old and not really suitable for such a rigorous service. Their other 'continental' steamers, including the old *Swift* and *Swallow*, had been withdrawn and sold some years earlier. The General Steam Navigation Company looked carefully at recent technological developments in engineering and chose a radical new design that they hoped would capture public acclaim in the way that the *Lord of the Isles* had some fifteen years earlier. Their new vessel was to be revolutionary in that it was to be the first propeller driven, turbine excursion steamer to operate on the Thames.

The steam turbine had been developed by the engineer Charles Parsons during 1894 and in that same year he had built a small experimental vessel named *Turbinia*. After initial disappointment, a modification to the propellers doubled *Turbinia*'s speed to a staggering thirty knots! In an effort to interest the Admiralty, Parsons laid on an unscheduled demonstration of *Turbinia* at the 1897 Jubilee

Review at Spithead. Nobody could fail to be impressed with this little vessel as she sped past the fastest naval vessels in the world! It is not surprising that *Turbinia* was always a popular attraction on the occasions when she put into Great Yarmouth. Also, such a fast and efficient means of propulsion could not help but interest steamship operators whose overheads were continually rising.

Denny's had been at the forefront of turbine steamer construction when in 1901 they had combined with Parsons to build the world's first commercial turbine steamship. Named *King Edward*, she was built for use on the Clyde. In case the new means of propulsion proved a failure, Denny's placed clearly visible marks on the deck where traditional paddle boxes could be placed! In the event, paddles were not required and, by economically averaging nineteen knots in service, *King Edward* achieved great success. Denny's quickly established a reputation for turbine steamer construction and therefore it was not surprising that the General Steam Navigation Company approached the Dumbarton shipyard for their new vessel which was to be named *Kingfisher*.

With a new vessel being built, the General Steam Navigation Company started to streamline their fleet and the first casualty was the other 'Kingfisher', the old *Halcyon*. After a busy season in 1904, which took her to Great Yarmouth on numerous occasions, she was withdrawn. In the summer of 1905 she appeared on the south coast sailing for the South of England Steamboat Company. However, that Company went out of business at the end of 1905 and, probably, because of a clause in the agreement of sale, *Halcyon* was bought back by the General Steam Navigation Company. She was to appear in Great Yarmouth for the last time during August 1906 and after the close of the season was again sold, to German interests who ran her on the River Elbe as *Cuxhaven*. The ultimate fate of this regular visitor to Great Yarmouth is unknown but she was probably scrapped soon after the Great War.

While their rivals looked to the future the Coast Development Corporation were involved with the present and with developments at Felixstowe. The Corporation's new pier was opened to the public on July 1st 1905 although, by all accounts, the structure was at least a month away from completion. Railings had yet to be fixed along its entire length and the number of seats provided stopped well short of the pier head. Visitors were left to squat on the baulks of timber that were left lying about. However, it seems that they were quite content to ''take the sea air'' and watch the boats come and go. The first vessel to berth was the *Woolwich Belle* on her way from Ipswich to Walton and Clacton. To signal her arrival Captain Holland fired a rocket gun several times and this it is said ''brought people all over Felixstowe to their feet'' thinking that a Russian squadron was bearing down on the town. (Readers may recall that this was a period when Russia was viewed with great suspicion and tension ran high. During the previous Autumn the so-called 'outrage' had taken place when a Russian naval squadron, *en route* to the Pacific, had shelled a number of Hull fishing boats.) *Walton Belle* was the next vessel to berth and yet more rockets were fired but, without the effect of those earlier! When completed, the New Pier (as it was known) was lit by electric lamps and, like that at Walton-on-the-Naze, was provided with an electric tramway running along its north side. The open-sided, 'toast-rack' vehicles proved very popular and saved passengers a walk of over half a mile to the pier head. Both of these features greatly added to the piers charm and to the 'romantic' nature of many of *Woolwich Belle*'s evening excursions.

Captain Holland brings Woolwich Belle *alongside Felixstowe New Pier for the first time on July 1st 1905.*

Felixstowe New Pier was the last pier to be built by the Belle Steamers. *It was opened in July 1905 and like the similar construction at Walton-on-the-Naze, had a tramway running along its north side.*

Three days after the opening celebrations at Felixstowe, the Corporation were reminded one of the cruelty of the sea by a macabre discovery off Southwold. While fishing off the town, Henry Green found a badly decomposed body floating about half a mile from the shore. Because of the nature of the body he was unable to get it into his boat and instead towed it to the beach. There it was identified from a guernsey as being that of Joseph Carter, a seaman who had fallen overboard from the *Walton Belle* in June.

This incident had occurred while *Walton Belle* was running her early season daily shuttle service between Great Yarmouth and Walton. As usual, this became a daily service to London in early July, when *Walton Belle*, supported by either *Yarmouth Belle* or *Southwold Belle* ran the long east coast service, one vessel up and one vessel down each day. However, with the improvements at Felixstowe, the Corporation decided to open a new Sunday express service by sending *Southend Belle* to Felixstowe. The vessel left London Bridge in the morning, stopping only at Tilbury for the benefit of rail passengers, before running straight through to Felixstowe. She arrived at the New Pier early in the afternoon and left again at 4.00 p.m. so giving passengers time to "form their ideas of the resort". This service was obviously regarded by the Corporation as rather special, for only saloon tickets were issued and a special dinner was also served in the dining room at 6.00 p.m.

While the services provided by the *Belle* Steamers remained constant during the first half of the Edwardian period, the number and variety of excursions offered to the holiday-maker continued to grow. Even with two vessels engaged on the Great Yarmouth service, one to Kent and one, or pehaps two to Walton, the Corporation still had sufficient vessels to be flexible enough to offer numerous day trips as well as having vessels available for charter.

Chartering a '*Belle*' for the day was popular with London businesses as the list of charters for 1908 shows. These outings usually ran from London Bridge to Clacton or Margate although this was not always the case. One of the most unusual charters was that by the 'Ancient Order of Druids' who arrived at Clacton in July 1906 and, I can only trust that they had a good journey! Unfortunately I have been unable to find the cost of hiring a vessel for the day.

Charters and excursions from Great Yarmouth were always difficult with the daily steamer arriving late one day and leaving early the next. The sea trips provided by the local paddle tugs were understandably popular and competition with them impossible unless an extra vessel was to have been based in Great Yarmouth. As this was not practicable, the *Belle* Steamers did all they could to promote day trips using the daily 'down' steamer. Excursionists could enjoy a number of hours ashore at either Lowestoft, Southwold, Felixstowe or Walton and were on occasions given the opportunity to return in "the famous *London Belle*". These 'occasions' usually coincided with periods of heavy demand which naturally warranted the use of the large *London Belle* on the Great Yarmouth service. The use of the daily boat service to provide sea trips for excursionists was also seen in Kent. During 1906 *Southend Belle* and *Yarmouth Belle* were both advertised as providing excursions to Ramsgate and Herne Bay, the latter requiring the passengers to return by rail. Visitors to the Kent resorts were also provided with a range of day excursions to Clacton, Walton and, occasionally on Tuesdays, to Felixstowe. The shorter services provided by the *Woolwich Belle* from Ipswich allowed considerable time for a wide range of excursions from nearby resorts and

BELLE STEAMER EXCURSIONS.

LIST OF CHARTERS.

Through the kindness of Mr. S. J. R. Legerton (piermaster), we give below a list of the excursions to Clacton by the Belle steamers :—

June 22nd, Thames Police, Southend Belle, Clacton and Walton.

June 29th, "Daily Mirror," Southend Belle, Clacton.

July 2nd, N.E. London Licensed Victuallers, Southwold Belle, Clacton.

July 8th, Blackheath Licensed Victuallers, Yarmouth Belle, Clacton.

July 8th, Hackney Carriage Proprietors, Southend Belle, Clacton and Walton.

July 9th, East London Licensed Victuallers, Yarmouth Belle, Clacton.

July 13th, Royal Ancient Order of Buffaloes, Southend Belle, Clacton.

July 14th, Greenwich Conservative Club, Yarmouth Belle, Clacton and Walton.

July 14th, Pearl Life Assurance Company, Southwold Belle, Clacton.

July 22nd, National Deposit Friendly Society, Southend Belle, Clacton, Walton and Felixstowe.

July 28th, Sobjoit's excursion, Southwold Belle, Clacton.

August 19th, Ancient Order of Foresters, Yarmouth Belle, Clacton and Walton

It is with sincere regret that we announce the death of Mr. W. A. Tanner, one of the directors of Tanner and Co., Ltd., paper merchants, Salisbury Square, Fleet Street, which took place very suddenly on Sunday last. A gentleman of unswerving integrity, he was highly respected by those whose good fortune it was to be brought into contact with him, and those whose business relations were confined to correspondence regarded him with that esteem that a tried and trusted friend shows to another. The funeral took place at Caterham Cemetery on Thursday.

THE BELLE STEAMERS.

NOTICE.

The BELLE STEAMERS now stop at

Gorleston

Daily for

LOWESTOFT, SOUTHWOLD, FELIXSTOWE, & WALTON.

Booking Office for Tickets and further particulars of **Mr. H. Lee**, Tobacconist, Opposite Tramway Depôt.

This advert from the Yarmouth Mercury of July 29th 1905 advertises the new stopping place at Gorleston. Harry Lee was the Belle Steamers' local agent.

A crowded Southend Belle unloads passengers at Gorleston after the trip from London. Belle Steamers stopped regularly at Gorleston after 1905 mainly because of pressure from the Coast Development Corporation local agent and other interested parties.

Belle Steamer loading Passengers at Gorleston-on-Sea.

those offered in 1906 were typical of the period. Other excursions to Southwold and Lowestoft were also advertised from Ipswich but it is doubtful if these were ever run by the *Woolwich Belle* for, although she was a good seaboat and often crossed the Thames estuary, I've seldom found evidence of her presence north of Aldeburgh. Perhaps the Corporation felt that a larger, faster vessel would be more appropriate. Instead, *Clacton Belle* was widely used together with the more modern *Southend Belle* and *Southwold Belle*. Passengers from Ipswich were transferred at Felixstowe New Pier for the journey up the coast and on arrival at Lowestoft were given an hour ashore while the steamer lay at the Claremont Pier. Those passengers opting to visit Southwold were given up to two and a half hours ashore.

The new General Steam Navigation Company's turbine steamer, *Kingfisher*, came into service in May 1906. With a speed of over twenty knots she was certainly an impressive vessel but, unfortunately for her owners, the impression she caused along the Thames was not altogether what they had wanted. Like her cross-channel predecessor *La Marguerite*, the *Kingfisher* was followed by a large wash that gave rise to numerous complaints from other river users. It was also found that *Kingfisher* was surprisingly difficult to manoeuvre alongside the piers. This was as much due to the nature of these piers as to the vessels' inherent lack of manoeuvreability compared to that of a traditional paddle steamer. Unlike stone jetties, piers are not solid structures. The piles allow the tide to flow through unimpeded and any vessel coming alongside is always liable to experience the effect of a freak wave or surge of tide. To the highly manoeuvrable paddle steamer this caused few problems but to *Kingfisher* it was a different matter. Parson's had discovered during experiments with the *Turbinia* that small, high-speed propellers of the type fitted to *Kingfisher*, had the tendency to allow small air bubbles to form on the propeller blades and this, in effect, meant that the blades were not in contact with the water, a phenomenon now known as 'cavitation'. It was, however, not really noticeable to those aboard when *Kingfisher* was going forwards at speed but, if 'hard astern' was suddenly called, as frequently happened when approaching piers, the propellers slipped and the vessel took a considerable time to come to a stop. Fortunately none of the piers visited by *Kingfisher* had side berths where the vessel would have been in danger of running up onto a beach! However, cavitation was to be a problem that bedevilled the vessel throughout its Thames career and, along with other problems, probably resulted in the paddle-wheel remaining the most popular means of propulsion until the 1930's.

Kingfisher's services were to stretch all along the Kent Coast and across the Channel but never to my knowledge further north than Southend. Certainly, if such a fast vessel had been employed on the Great Yarmouth service, it would have proved very popular. This route was fast becoming uneconomic for the General Steam Navigation Company as by 1906 stops along the East Coast were essential if a profit was to be made. Even The General Steam Navigation Company could no longer boast a direct service as they now regularly off-loaded passengers into small boats near Lowestoft harbour. It was all they could do in an effort to make their service more attractive.

With *Kingfisher* running to Kent, the need to maintain the old 'Classical Birds' was further reduced. However, in 1907, the four remaining vessels still ran the East Coast service although, it was said, none could make more than thirteen

79

knots! At the end of the season Philomel was withdrawn and sold to the Lancashire based Furness Railway Company. By all accounts she had never been a popular ship in Great Yarmouth, probably because of her speed, and, we are told that the sight of her distinctive funnel at South Quay brought a sigh from prospective passengers. *Philomel* was to continue services in Morecambe Bay until 1913, when she was sold for scrap.

The *Belle* Steamers would not have been particularly concerned if *Philomel* had not been withdrawn, such was their dominance of the East Coast services. Indeed, their range of excursions from the Essex resorts were as extensive as those provided in 1906. The only set-back to their services in 1907 came in September when *Southwold Belle* suffered paddle wheel damage after a collision in dense fog off Tilbury.

By 1908, The General Steam Navigation Company had decided to maintain their Great Yarmouth service but to concentrate further on their Kent services by replacing the remaining 'Classical Birds' with a new vessel. Experience with the *Kingfisher* had shown that a fast turbine steamer sailed less effectively on the confined waters of the Thames than on the 'open' Clyde. It was therefore decided to order a traditional paddle steamer of a similar size to *Kingfisher* and to have this new vessel ready for service in 1909.

As the maintenance of the Great Yarmouth service did not require three vessels, the first casualty of this rationalisation was *Laverock*. In 1908 she was sold to the French, Compagnie Maritime of Bordeaux, who renamed her *Ville de Royan* for services in the Gironde estuary.

The General Steam Navigation Company's new paddle steamer, named *Golden Eagle*, came into service in the summer of 1909. Built by John Brown and Company of Clydebank, she had been beautifully fitted out and given a full length promenade deck. Once on the Thames she joined *Eagle* on the run to Margate and Ramsgate and very soon built up a considerable reputation for comfort and reliability. *Kingfisher* maintained her Boulogne services on Monday and Thursday; a timetable that allowed her other days to compete with *Koh-i-Noor* on the service to Dover. Indeed, she was timetabled to leave Margate shortly before her arrival!

Into this intense competition the *Belle* Steamers sent *London Belle*. She was time-tabled for an excursion from Margate to Ramsgate before returning to London at 3.30 p.m. Her appearance seems only to be a token gesture, as she could not possibly have hoped to compete with *Royal Sovereign* which left Margate on exactly the same services a few minutes earlier. *Woolwich Belle* was also timetabled to sail from Margate on Wednesdays for Clacton, Walton, Felixstowe and Harwich. This was a single trip, the return half of an excursion from the Essex coast.

Woolwich Belle's regular appearance in Kent resulted from a major reorganisation of her services. From the beginning of July 1909, *Woolwich Belle* was withdrawn from Ipswich. Although this was ostensibly due to berthing problems, it was also felt that the Orwell service was not as profitable as the longer excursions made possible if the steamer were to be based at Felixstowe. For this reason *Woolwich Belle* was once again sent to the Great Eastern Railway's pier at the mouth of the Orwell, and placed on a wide variety of excursions including return trips to Margate, Tilbury, Herne Bay and Strood. Her services were still advertised from Ipswich but passengers were taken by train from Derby Road Station to Felixstowe's Riverside pier. Only on Tuesday did *Woolwich Belle* venture up the

Orwell to Ipswich. These changes broke with a tradition begun in 1894 but, surprisingly, hardly a mention was made of it in contemporary newspapers. How different this was from the detailed accounts that were published of *Woolwich Belle* first services.

The only other change affecting the *Belle* Steamers was the withdrawal of the *Mavis*. In August 1909, she was sold to Pockett's Bristol Channel Steam Packet Company for whom she sailed until 1915 when she was scrapped. The withdrawal of *Mavis* left only one 'Classical Bird', *Oriole*, available for the East Coast service, thus preventing the maintenance of a daily service. This, and the record numbers reported landed at Lowestoft's Claremont Pier in late July, prompted the Corporation to send a special *Belle* Steamer to Lowestoft on the 1909 Bank Holiday Saturday.

In spite of their gradual withdrawal from the long East Coast service, in 1910 the General Steam Navigation Company returned to Great Yarmouth with *Oriole*. It was a limited service and could not have been very profitable. Her appearance in the Yare over the August Bank Holiday seems to have been that of 'showing the flag' as the East Coast service was already well catered for by *Southwold Belle*, *Clacton Belle* and *Walton Belle*.

Along the Kent coast it was quite a different story as *Golden Eagle* was proving immensely popular, even threatening the position of *Royal Sovereign* as London's favourite steamer. The appearance of *Southwold Belle*, *Yarmouth Belle* and *Woolwich Belle* at Margate could make little effect on the services provided by New Palace Steamers and The General Steam Navigation Company and, probably added to the Corporation's growing financial crisis.

This crisis had been gradually developing throughout the previous decade and was due to a number of factors. As the Corporation's routes had been concentrated along the east coast north of the Thames, they naturally found themselves maintaining long routes and, as we have seen the profitability of these routes was constantly threatened by developments to the road network, the rail system and by changing public attitudes. To some extent, *Belle* Steamers were encumbered by unprofitable services in the same way as early Thames steamboat companies. Readers must remember that profit made during the season had to maintain the vessel throughout the eight months they remained idle! The General Steam Navigation Company had realised these problems and, as we have seen, had focused their attention on the shorter, always profitable Kent routes for a number of years. Perhaps this lack of foresight on the part of the Corporation was another example of their poor management during the Edwardian period. It may also have been that *Belle* Steamers did not keep financial control over catering on their vessels, preferring instead to lease it to outside caterers. If this were the case, then large profits were being lost as catering provided much more income than ticket sales! Also, it is important to realise that the Coast Development Corporation's financial stability depended on far more than revenue from steamships. They were landowners, Edwardian land speculators and as so often happens in the speculative market, projects do not always go as planned. Indeed, some of their land was reported lost through coastal erosion! By 1911 a large number of mortgages had been taken out and the Corporation had a significant number of liabilities to meet.

In early June 1911 the *Belle* Steamers were advertised as the ''Belle Line — the

After the failure of the Kingfisher *The General Steam Navigation Company returned to paddle propulsion with the popular* Golden Eagle *in 1909.*

In this postcard published by Belle Steamers, *Woolwich Belle is shown after having her telescopic funnel replaced by one of a fixed design. Later the foresaloon was extended and the distinctive set of steps was removed. This made her a much more comfortable sea boat.*

Mr. George Riley
(Chairman of the Coast Development Corporation), as seen by our Cartoonist.

Company Chairman George Riley as seen in the East Coast Illustrated News in September 1909. By this date it is doubtful if anybody could have steered the Corporation back towards financial solvency without major changes.

The paddle steamer Mavis *is here seen at Bristol after her sale to Pockett's Bristol Channel Steam Packet Company in 1909.*

only passenger steamers between London and Great Yarmouth''. The General Steam Navigation Company had earlier announced their complete withdrawal from this route, enabling them to use *Oriole* as a reserve boat on the Thanet services. For the first time in history, *Belle* Steamers possessed a complete monopoly of the steamboat services between Southend and Great Yarmouth. However, it soon proved a hollow success.

During the summer season, the *Belle Line* embarked on a number of new services in an attempt to maximise their profits. One of these was an express return service from Great Yarmouth to Tilbury stopping only at Lowestoft. For this popular Saturday service a variety of vessels was used including the large *London Belle*. Although *Walton Belle* was based in Great Yarmouth from early June, she did not start a daily service to Walton until early July. 1911 is one of the few years when, so far as I can see, *Walton Belle* was seldom used on the east coast service. For an unknown reason she seldom appeared in Great Yarmouth after mid-July and no one vessel could be said to have maintained the daily service.

A possible explanation is that *Walton Belle* may have been used for services along the Kent coast in conjunction with *Woolwich Belle*. However, whatever the services provided, by the end of the season, financial problems had become acute and required immediate action. With debts mounting and a large coal bill unpaid, the Corporation decided to reduce their overheads and raise capital by selling one of their vessels.

The decision as to which steamer to sell was not quite as simple as at first appears. The obvious candidate was the oldest vessel, *Clacton Belle*. But, from the experiences of The General Steam Navigation Company, old vessels would not raise much cash. Few major paddle steamer operators required steamers let alone older ones! The only vessel likely to arouse interest would be the newer *Southwold Belle*. So, reluctantly, the decision was made. *Southwold Belle* paid her last visit to Southwold Pier on September 23rd 1911 and at the end of the season was withdrawn and offered for sale. There were no British buyers and eventually *Southwold Belle* was purchased by the German, Hamburg-America Line for use as tender and was renamed *Westerland*. A year later she was resold to French interests and renamed *Bon Voyage* for use at Cherbourg. There she was to remain until the Great War. In 1922 she was sold to Societa Anonima Pragma and registered at Genoa. During 1924 she was transferred to Vasala & Narizzano who had her dismantled in 1925. *Southwold Belle* was the last *Belle* Steamer to have been built and sadly, perhaps prematurely, the first to be scrapped.

But *Southwold Belle* was not the only Thames vessel to be sold after the 1911 season. The General Steam Navigation Company decided to reduce their fleet by selling *Kingfisher*. Although the *Oriole* was much older, *Kingfisher* had never been a great success and after the initial interest aroused, the vessels' popularity had waned. Indeed, she is said to have been a 'lively seaboat', causing much distress to passengers in a "lumpy" sea. Her only claim to fame is that she is reputed to have carried Crippen and his mistress across the Channel. In 1912 she was sold to Italian interests and taken to Trieste where she was renamed *Venezia*. *Kingfisher* remained in the Adriatic until 1928 after which she embarked on a nomadic existence that ended in Hong Kong during 1938.

The sale of *Southwold Belle* and the essential financial restraints did not reduce the *Belle* Steamer services. Passengers in 1912 would not have noticed any major

CHERBOURG. — La Gare Maritime, — LL.

Bon Voyage *(ex-*Southwold Belle*) is at Cherbourg just before the Great War. This is just one of a number of French postcards that depict paddle steamers in ports along the Channel coast.*

changes — only an increasing reputation for lateness! Indeed, they may have been amused by the "New Clacton Belle Sea Song" written by Robert Coan. The Corporation had paid twenty guineas for the rights to play and sing this song on their piers and steamers. Unfortunately I've not been able to find the words to the song but I'm sure that by the end of the season it must have seemed very monotonous to regular pier users! The song didn't help the Corporation's finances and with the railway offering reduced return fares from London to Clacton, Walton and Great Yarmouth, the Corporation found it hard to compete. Ironically, the late August hurricane-force winds that destroyed the *Belle* Steamer ticket office at Gorleston quay and battered *Yarmouth Belle*, causing so much distress to her passengers, also flooded the railway network near Great Yarmouth. Anxious passengers inquiring at South Town Station were advised to take the 9.15 a.m. steamer to Felixstowe! This is the only time I have read of this happening. However, the sudden boost to trade did not really help the Corporation and at the beginning of September they announced in the press that they were going to finish their sailings a week earlier than intended. The last boat from Great Yarmouth, *Walton Belle*, sailed for London on September 10th 1912.

1912 also saw the sale of the final 'Classical Bird'. The old *Oriole* was towed from Deptford to new owners in Holland where she ended her days as a hulk. Where and when she was scrapped is unknown.

During 1913, as political events in Europe took their course, the *Belle* Steamers continued running to all the resorts along the east coast and, although venturing to Kent, they preferred to visit towns avoided by their competitors. In this way the Corporation managed to extract a profit, keep their fleet intact and their creditors at bay.

The services for 1914 reflect the intensive and wide-ranging use to which the *Belle* Steamer fleet was put to during this time of developing crisis. The East Coast services continued as before with vessels from London to Walton via Clacton and to Great Yarmouth sailing daily. One major change was that *Woolwich Belle* was based on alternate weeks at Sheerness. From there she sailed a variety of services including trips to Ipswich, Herne Bay, Margate and Rochester. On Fridays she would return light to London in order to run the Saturday morning service to Felixstowe and Harwich. During the next week she would be based at Harwich leaving her former service from Sheerness to *Walton Belle*. Whilst at Harwich, *Woolwich Belle* ran excursions to Margate, Southwold, Lowestoft and Rochester before returning to London on Saturday morning. From there she went to Sheerness and took over *Walton Belle* services of the previous week. The two steamers alternated in this manner throughout the season, a season that was destined to be brought to a premature end.

Belles at War — 1914 to 1920 5

Throughout the early part of the summer of 1914 the *Belle Line*'s east coast services were as extensive as they had been in previous years and, with the good weather, that summer promised to be a splendid season. Then, the world events that had dominated the newspapers for many months culminated with a declaration of war on August 4th 1914. On that fateful day the services along the east coast sailed as advertised, with *Yarmouth Belle* setting out from Great Yarmouth in the morning and *Clacton Belle* arriving that evening. With war imminent, the small crowd that watched *Clacton Belle*'s arrival at Haven Bridge must have wondered if they were witnessing the last of the *Belle* Steamers. And, had they been aware of events then taking place in the North Sea less than sixty miles away, they would have had even more reason for such thoughts.

With war inevitable, the German navy had requisitioned a number of merchant ships of which one, the excursion vessel *Königen Luise* had been fitted out for mine laying in just twelve hours. This twin-funnelled vessel strongly resembled ships of the Great Eastern Railway's fleet that ran from Harwich to the Hook of Holland and, to increase the likelihood of her being mistaken for one of these packet-ships, she was even painted in Great Eastern Railway's colours. In the early hours of August 5th, while the *Clacton Belle* was safely moored in Great Yarmouth, *Königen Luise* was busy laying mines in the shipping lanes South East of Aldeburgh. Unfortunately, the summer rain squall that had covered her approach lifted briefly and she was seen by a fishing vessel apparently ''throwing things overboard''. A little later this trawler encountered the destroyers *H.M.S. Landrail* and *H.M.S. Lance* which, as part of the 2nd Destroyer Flotilla, had left Harwich at dawn for their first wartime patrol. The strange behaviour of the ''two-funnelled vessel'' was reported and the warships steamed off to investigate followed by the light cruiser *H.M.S. Amphion* and other vessels of the flotilla. The destroyers encountered the *Königen Luise* some twenty miles north east of the Outer Gabbard while she was still minelaying. There was little the Germans could do as the destroyers approached because their vessel's conversion had been so quick, that the intended 3.4 inch guns had not been fitted. The only answer they had to the first shells of the Great War was small arms fire. Their situation was hopeless and, after a surprisingly lengthy chase, the German Captain decided to scuttle his vessel to avoid needless waste of life. As *Königen Luise* rolled over and disappeared, the British warships stopped to pick up survivors before continuing with their North Sea patrol. It was mid-day and further west the *Clacton Belle*, packed with returning Londoners steamed past Aldeburgh out of earshot of the gunfire but within sight of the German minefield — a minefield that the following morning was to claim the lives of 151 British sailors when the cruiser *H.M.S. Amphion* was sunk on her way back to Harwich. By a strange twist of irony, at least eighteen German survivors from *Königen Luise* were also killed when the forepart of the cruiser was shattered by the explosion. Thus, mines were soon seen as a great threat to coastal shipping and as a counter-measure the Admiralty resorted to an earlier contingency plan and requisitioned fishing trawlers to search for them. The first of these minesweepers were in service by the end of August 1914.

In spite of this very great threat, the East Coast summer service continued with daily boats to Clacton and Great Yarmouth running as usual. Indeed, as the number of passengers returning to London increased after the Bank Holiday, there was a need for more capacity. Consequently, on Saturday August 8th, two steamers *Yarmouth Belle* and *Southend Belle*, sailed from Great Yarmouth amid much cheering and choruses of *God Save the King*. The clerk in the quayside office took great pride in announcing to anxious enquiries that "the services are being continued exactly as usual". Very little attention was paid to the war and it seems incredible that with mines and the increasing U-boat menace, announcements were still being made in the Press as to just when and where vessels were sailing! It was not until August 18th that newspapers "regretfully" announced they were no longer giving details of shipping movements. The only tangible gesture made by the *Belle* Steamers to the war was that all passengers had to give in writing, their name, age, sex, occupation and destination before boarding the steamers. With our hindsight this does not seem surprising, but a postcard written on August 21st by a lady boarding the *Walton Belle* at Walton for the trip to Lowestoft, shows what seems a degree of surprise at such demands. Nevertheless, these details led to the detention of two Germans at Great Yarmouth after they had taken passage on the *Clacton Belle*.

Elsewhere the war seemed much closer. Even before the outbreak of hostilities, Dover harbour had been closed to pleasure steamers and when *Koh-i-Noor* had arrived there for the last time on July 30th, we are told that she seemed "to be the only unarmed vessel in that vast expanse of enclosed water". On August 10th Ramsgate's East Pier, where the paddle steamers usually berthed, was requisitioned and closed. From this date services from London terminated at Margate. The General Steam Navigation Company soon decided to withdraw the *Eagle* while New Palace Steamers took the opportunity to send *Koh-i-Noor* to her builders for a long overdue refit. Sadly for this magnificent vessel the needs of war prevented the planned work from starting. After numerous delays *Koh-i-Noor* was towed across the Clyde to Gareloch where she was laid up and forgotten until almost the end of the hostilities. Throughout August requisitioned vessels sailed past Felixstowe and into Harwich, one of the first being the Great Yarmouth paddle tug *King Edward VII* which, on August 1st, had left for an "unspecified term of engagement".

Southend Belle left Great Yarmouth for the last time on September 16th and from then until the close of the season, the east coast service was left in the hands of both *Walton Belle* and *Yarmouth Belle*, which ran to Walton on the usual shuttle service. According to the port records, the final departure from Great Yarmouth came on the morning of Monday, August 31st when, some weeks before the usual close of the season, *Walton Belle* had sailed for London and an uncertain future. Both *Golden Eagle* and *Royal Sovereign* probably ran along the Kent coast until the normal end of the season in mid-September, then they too were laid up.

Unlike the General Steam Navigation Company or Fairfields, the owners of *Royal Sovereign*, the Coast Development Corporation were severely stretched financially and with their future income now in jeopardy their creditors were naturally nervous. The war did not end as people had hoped at Christmas 1914 and, as it intensified during the early months of 1915, it became increasingly obvious to the Corporation that no summer services would be required. Without any trade there was no income and no way of meeting their heavy liabilities. At an extra-ordinary General Meeting held on May 21st 1915, it was decided that under the circumstances, the Corporation could no longer continue trading and that, regretfully, it should go into voluntary liquidation. On 7th June, 1915, A. F. Whinney and J. F. Stovell were appointed as liquidators to deal with the Corporation's assets and numerous creditors. By this date all the steamships and much of the property owned by the Corporation had mortgages raised on them. In many ways the liquidation of the Coast Development Corporation in 1915 marks a watershed in our story. For, although some of the vessels were to sail again in post war years with the same name, and even the same flag, the roots of the company that stretched back through such worthy characters as Horace Spence, Abel Penfold and Peter Bruff, were cleanly severed. *Belle* Steamers were never to be the same. But, there again, so much of the 'old order' was changing in 1915.

The General Steam Navigation Company experienced this 'change' at first hand when in February 1915 the Admiralty requisitioned the *Golden Eagle* for troop transportation. On February 23rd 1915 she left Southampton for Rouen with some 698 soldiers aboard. It was to be the first of many such journeys. Perhaps her most unusual passengers were landed at Southampton on March 13th. These were 569 Germans who had been captured during the bitter fighting at Neuve Chapelle. Four days later *Golden Eagle* was joined on her Channel trips by the old Thames favourite *La Marguerite*, which as a troop carrier was in her element; after all there was no need to economise on speed or worry about the wash!

Troop transportation was of great importance but, in early 1915, the Admiralty was concerned with more urgent matters. The mine threat had not abated and the trawlers requisitioned for minesweeping duties were suffering heavy losses. It has since been estimated that during 1914 one minesweeper was sunk for every five mines destroyed and, at least one vessel of some sort was lost for every two mines destroyed. Quite obviously such losses couldn't continue. It was simply that the needs of a fishing trawler were not those of a minesweeper! Fishing required slow speeds and a robust, deep-draughted vessel. The deadly contact mines that were being scattered throughout the North Sea required a minesweeper that was fast and preferably had a shallow draught. The German mines were usually anchored at various depths below the surface by a stout wire cable. Minesweeping required these cables to be cut so that the mine would float to the surface where it could be safely destroyed by rifle fire. One of the most common methods of doing this, employed during World War I, was to pair two trawlers together with a wire hawser stretched between them. This hawser was intended to sever the mine cable but, unfortunately, the slow speeds of the trawlers often resulted in the cable remaining intact. The mine then became ensnared in the minesweeping gear, often with disastrous results for the nearest trawler. The Admiralty was forced to search for alternative vessels and their attention fell on the redundant paddle steamers to be found lying idle in ports around our coast.

Indeed, the Admiralty had expressed an interest in the shallow draught and comparatively fast excursion paddle steamers in early September 1914. During that month they selected P & A Campbell's *Brighton Queen* and *Devonia* for an extensive series of minesweeping trials which, by December 1914, had proved very successful. From that date suitable paddle steamers were requisitioned for minesweeping duties.

On August 6th 1915 both *Clacton Belle* and *Yarmouth Belle* were taken into Admiralty service. Within about six weeks the two steamers were dramatically altered. The rich, ornate saloons and day cabins were gutted and their contents stored for use at a later date. A small deckhouse was constructed to house a wireless and its operator while a new, shorter, second mast was fitted aft of the bridge to accommodate the aerials. The bridge remained behind the funnel but had a navigation house and chart-room added to it. The main saloons were transformed by numerous divisions into cabins while a large space was left as an officers' mess. The large windows and smaller port-holes were plated over for safety. Below, the empty dining rooms were gradually filled with all the spare equipment required by a minesweeper including the ammunition for the guns that were fitted. These included a 6 lb. Hotchkiss automatic anti-submarine gun fixed to the top of a raised platform forward, and a 6 lb. high-angle anti-aircraft gun mounted aft. (An aerial attack had already been experienced by the crew of the paddle minesweeper *Albyn* when their vessel was damaged by a German seaplane in August 1915.) The minesweeping gear was fitted aft and comprised a large steel gantry erected over the stern. Alongside this was a huge 9 ton winch on which was wound approximately 250 yds. of steel hawser used for lowering the nets, floats and sinkers used in sweeping. Searchlights were fitted to the forepart of the promenade deck to aid minesweeping at night. But, after the destruction of *Brighton Queen* during a night sweeping experiment off Newport in October 1915, the *Belles* were ordered to sweep during daylight hours only. To enable the vessels to remain at sea for the longer periods of time required by the Admiralty, additional bunkers were constructed to store up to 80 tons of extra coal. With modifications complete, and freshly painted in regulation Admiralty Grey, the *Yarmouth Belle*, now *H.M.P.M.S. 929*, and *Clacton Belle*, *H.M.P.M.S. 930*, proceeded to Sheerness to commence duties.

The next Thames paddle steamer to be requisitioned was the *Eagle*, which renamed *Aiglon*, commenced minesweeping in the North Sea on November 22nd 1915. A week later *Yarmouth Belle* narrowly escaped destruction. While minesweeping near The Galloper, her partner, the Scottish paddle steamer *Duchess of Hamilton*, struck a mine. The explosion shattered the lightly built steamer and she quickly began to settle. Although damaged by the blast, the *Yarmouth Belle* approached the stricken vessel and plucked the few lucky survivors from the freezing North Sea. By a strange twist of irony the *Duchess of Hamilton* was being built by Denny's at the same time as the *Clacton Belle* in 1890.

Losses continued to mount and P & A Campbell again suffered when their paddle steamer *Lady Ismay* blew up near the Longsands Lightvessel on December 21st 1915. The following day *Walton Belle* was requisitioned and quickly converted in the manner already outlined. She joined her sisters in their perilous occupation as *H.M.P.M.S. 579*. *London Belle* was requisitioned on March 19th 1916 and was shortly followed by the *Southend Belle* on April 2nd. They were respectively numbered *H.M.P.M.S. 530* and *H.M.P.M.S. 532*. *Woolwich Belle* was not requisitioned, and like *Royal Sovereign* its exact use during the war is unknown. Although unconfirmed, both vessels probably remained in London throughout the hostilities. Like the British Government, the French also used paddle steamers in a variety of military roles. *Bon Voyage*, the former *Southwold Belle*, was sent to the Mediterranean where amongst other duties she was used to transport troops.

The wartime crew of a *Belle* Steamer numbered about forty. They were provided by the Admiralty and were usually Naval Reservists from the Merchant Marine. A few of the Corporation's engineers were appointed to the minesweepers as they were familiar with the ships' machinery. None of the Captains that were so well known to peacetime passengers was employed, as their specialised knowledge of Thames waters made them excellent river pilots.

During 1916 all the *Belle* Steamers were stationed at Harwich and this was to remain their base until late 1917. It was during this period that the crew of the *Clacton Belle* had their first contact with the enemy in person. This happened when she helped to rescue sailors from a German airship which had crashed in the Thames Estuary. This was probably the Zeppelin L.15., which crashed in March 1916.

Although there were other rescues, most notably by *London Belle* from the *S.S. Peregrine* in December 1917, this was an exception. Generally speaking, life on a paddle minesweeper was grim, unexciting and highly dangerous. Their sinister enemy was unseen and death usually came without warning. Friends, there one moment, were gone in the next. There was seldom any chance of saving a ship, you just dragged as many survivors from the sea as you could, knowing all the time that the next second might be your last. In June 1917 the paddle minesweeper *Kempton* was blown up as she went to rescue the crew of her sister vessel *Redcar*, mined minutes earlier! It was frustrating work and has since been described as one-sided: "heads you win, tails I lose". The only tangible recognition of the heroism showed by the *Belle* Steamer crews during their period at Harwich was the award of the DSO to Commander Wegram of the *Yarmouth Belle* and Commander Sutton-Smith of the *Clacton Belle*. The *Clacton Belle* alone had been responsible for the destruction of no fewer than 342 mines in operations that stretched from the Thames to the Danish coast.

Although the Thames Estuary was not free of mines, the decision was taken in late 1917 to send *Southend Belle*, *Clacton Belle*, and *London Belle* to Liverpool. The reason for this was that the approaches to the River Mersey had become an increasingly popular target for submarine laid mines since the United States had entered the war in April 1917. The next eighteen months was to see the four steamers engaged in what was said at the time to be "exceptionally heavy work" which ranged from Cardigan Bay to the Isle of Man. *Walton Belle* did not join her sisters but went instead to the Tyne where her onerous duties continued into 1918.

By 1918 the surviving requisitioned minesweepers were being joined by an increasing number of purpose built vessels of which the "Ascot" class were paddle driven. It was a tribute to the effectiveness of all requisitioned paddle steamers that the Admiralty chose to base, if rather loosely, this new class of vessel on P & A Campbell's steamer *Glen Usk*.

As the war continued, a decision was made by Fairfields to dispose of its subsidiary company, New Palace Steamers, by selling their two remaining vessels. *Koh-i-Noor* had lain in Gareloch for almost four years and was in a poor condition. This fine steamer, once described as the "gem of the Thames", was sold for a mere £6,200 to Wards of Morecambe and scrapped. *Royal Sovereign* was lying at Tilbury, and as she had been re-boilered in 1913 was in a much better condition.

Bon Voyage (*ex-Southwold Belle*) *is seen disembarking French troops in the Mediterranean during the First World War. The photograph is thought to have been taken during the Gallipoli campaign.*

A photograph with the caption : ''6lb gun drill on the Walton Belle.*'' Were these four sailors the gun crew that won the anti-aircraft shooting prize? Sadly, their names are unrecorded and probably will never be known.*

But, who during wartime would buy a holiday excursion steamer? The answer was one Arthur William Pickard who, in March 1918, formed the Royal Sovereign Steamship Company. Pickard and his fellow directors were to play an important part in the post-war developments that affected the *Belle* Steamers.

The Great War officially ended on November 11th 1918 but mines had no respect for man's agreements and so the grim task of clearance continued into 1919. Such was the number of mines laid that the North Sea was not fully cleared until the summer of 1921. Although The General Steam Navigation Company's steamer *Golden Eagle* was returned in November 1919, the older *Eagle* remained under Admiralty orders until July 1920. The *Belle* Steamers returned somewhat earlier. According to their later owners, the first two vessels to leave active service were the *Southend Belle* and *Clacton Belle*. Both returned to Tilbury in March 1919 to be docked and reconditioned by the Admiralty. *London Belle* arrived at Tilbury during the first week of April after a non-stop run of 700 miles from Liverpool. After three years strenuous service she had still been able to average fifteen knots for the journey! *Yarmouth Belle* also arrived from Liverpool a few days later and both vessels were stripped of military equipment prior to reconditioning. *Walton Belle* probably returned from the Tyne in early May but she had not been back on the Thames for more than a week, when she and *London Belle* were re-requisitioned for further service.

Their new role was to be that of a Hospital Carrier and no sooner had the minesweeping equipment been dismantled than a large number of beds appeared on the quayside. Over 160 were destined for the *London Belle* alone! Such was the urgency that the fitting out of these two vessels continued day and night without stop. The hospital beds were fitted in the saloons while an operating theatre was constructed just aft of the main saloon. Some cabins were fitted out for surgeons and officers while others were converted into toilets. The fixings for a large canvas awning were placed so that the deck from the bridge to the paddle sponson rails could be shielded from the sun. Facilities improving ventilation and heating were also fitted. When finished, orders were received that made it clear why heating was required. *London Belle* and *Walton Belle*, now known as *H.C.2.* and *H.C.3.* respectively, were to proceed to the White Sea immediately. There they were to be used to convey soldiers wounded in the Russian campaign, down the Dvina River to a point where they could be transferred into larger ships for the journey home. The 2000 mile voyage to Russia took twenty days and must have been very challenging. The North Sea was particularly rough and the crews were glad to reach the Shetland Islands. After leaving Lerwick the ships made their way to Bergen and Hammerfest before rounding the inhospitable North Cape and sailing into Russian waters. Although I have been unable to find details of the voyage, we are told that the ships proved "thoroughly seaworthy".

Once they had arrived it became clear that little hospital work was to be done. Anyway, it was decided that the two ships would be much more gainfully employed transporting troops. It is interesting to note that during a major 'invasion exercise' on Clacton beach during the summer of 1904, the military had noticed how close the paddle steamers could come to the beach and had commented that this quality might, at a later date, prove useful. On the Dvina River it did, and, although records are sketchy, I am quite certain that both vessels came under fire on numerous occasions and sustained casualties. In one contemporary report we are told of an incident during which some Bolshevik prisoners escaped and attempted to take over the *Walton Belle*. Fortunately a merchant sailor appeared at the critical moment with a shot gun and killed two of the ringleaders. Order was then restored and *Walton Belle* continued with her task of transporting White Russian troops. Just where she was taking these troops is unclear, but we do have another report, this time from the Admiralty, that refers to the auxiliary paddle steamer *Walton Belle* accompanied by two monitors entering the Onega River to re-take the town of that name. *Walton Belle* was carrying a force of White Russians supported by British gunners who, after fierce fighting, withdrew leaving the town in Bolshevik control.

After about four months in the Arctic waters around Archangel, the two vessels returned to the Thames with, we are told, 'many impressions' from Maxim and snipers' guns on the funnel, ventilators and other parts of their superstructure. *Walton Belle* was released from Admiralty service in May 1920, and *London Belle* during July. Reconditioned and repainted, they joined *Southern Belle* (released 8th November 1919), *Clacton Belle* (released November 1919) and *Yarmouth Belle* (released 3rd January 1920) in the care of Whinney, Smith and Whinney, by then registered as the liquidators of the Coast Development Corporation.

Of the various paddle steamer fleets requisitioned for wartime service, the *Belle* fleet was one of the few that returned intact. This was as much through luck as the skill and courage shown by the nameless sailors who served in them. The Earl of Lytton speaking in the House of Lords in 1917, summed up the role of paddle minesweepers in the Great War. ''It is impossible to realise the magnificent and efficient work which was being done by the small craft engaged in sweeping the seas of mines sown broadcast by the enemy''.

The photograph of London Belle *was almost certainly taken while she was operating as a Hospital Ship in northern waters. It is possible that the picture was taken from the* Walton Belle.

A superb view of the Yarmouth Belle *in its role as minesweeper. The wheel for the bow rudder can clearly be seen at the forward end of the promenade deck. At the stern, the crew work with the large winch which was used to wind the sweeping cables.*

The Declining Years 6

The most complicated part of our story is that which follows the Great War. It was a period dominated by a few individuals and the numerous companies they created. Of these companies, records are either incomplete or simply don't exist. This lack of information has serious implications for the researcher as not all the important facts pertaining to the *Belle* Steamers are available. Without these facts I doubt if the whole story will ever be fully known and the development of *Belle* Steamers during the 1920's will always have question marks against it.

The story begins with the purchase of *Royal Sovereign* by A. W. Pickard in March 1918. With him in this speculative venture were two brothers, Robert Robertson Shankland and John Hamilton Shankland, both of whom, like Pickard, were ship-brokers. The company they formed on March 19th 1918 was registered as The Royal Sovereign Steamship Company. As it was still wartime their solicitor had to sign the Trading with the Enemy Act, 1914, thus guaranteeing that *Royal Sovereign* could not be used in activities considered prejudicial to the Crown. Two weeks later Pickard wrote to the Shankland brothers: ''We hereby agree to sell your company the *S.S. Royal Sovereign* together with her outfit according to Messrs. Kellocks' list for the sum of £10,000''. The vessel was to be paid for in 10,000 fully-paid one pound shares in the Shanklands' Company and presumably this compensated existing shareholders.

Exactly what ''your company'' refers to is unclear. It could refer to any one of a number of companies of which the Shankland brothers were co-directors and these include; Robert Shankland and Company, Shankland and Company (neither of which have left any records) and The General Maritime Trust. Unfortunately, I can find no references to the *Royal Sovereign* in any of them but I can assert that as *Royal Sovereign* had originally been purchased for £8,300, a handsome profit was made on this paper transaction! Without any assets the Royal Sovereign Steamship Company ceased trading and after a year it was voluntarily wound up, in April 1919. Where *Royal Sovereign* was, or exactly what the Shanklands had intended to use her for in 1918 is unrecorded. In May 1919 the Shanklands, Pickard and another former shareholder, Harold De Mattos, formed another company with the same name as the first, The Royal Sovereign Steamship Company! Of this second company we have very few details as records no longer exist but, certainly, *Royal Sovereign* appeared in May 1919 running a daily service from Old Swan Pier to Margate and was the first Thames pleasure steamer in service that summer.

While *Royal Sovereign* had been at the centre of these financial dealings, a proposal had been made by a Mr E. Kingsman of Clacton to charter a number of *Belle* Steamers from the liquidators. Kingsman intended to use the steamers on the usual services along the east coast, supporting various enterprises with which he was associated. *London Belle* and *Walton Belle* were still in the Arctic and *Clacton Belle*, *Southend Belle* and *Yarmouth Belle* had not yet been reconditioned. That left only *Woolwich Belle* and as she hadn't been used for almost five years, she wasn't considered.

In 1920 Mr Kingsman was more successful and chartered both *London Belle* and *Walton Belle* for east coast services. During August both steamers were in service, running daily, except Friday to their old haunts. *London Belle* ran from Fresh Wharf to Walton-on-the-Naze while *Walton Belle*, based in Great Yarmouth ran down the coast to meet her: "It is interesting to note that *Walton Belle* had been advertised to start service in July but, she did not pass her survey in time, she did not arrive in Great Yarmouth until August 4th". Advertisements encouraged visitors to have a "happy, healthy and thoughtful trip". Also, if they compared fares with those of the railways, passengers would not only save money but also 'temper'! The word 'thoughtful' probably reflects the publication of a booklet, sold aboard that told of the *Belle* Steamers' exploits during the Great War.

By the summer of 1921 Mr Kingsman had purchased many of the Coast Development Corporation assets including all the paddle steamers with the exception of *Woolwich Belle*. He had also purchased the five 'Belle Piers' but had quickly resold those at Walton, Felixstowe, Southwold and Lowestoft to local concerns, retaining only Clacton for which he had extensive plans. Land and other properties owned by the Coast Development Corporation were also sold about this time, including the Grand Hotel Southwold, which was auctioned during July 1921. *Woolwich Belle* was re-purchased by Denny's to be refitted and to provide employment in the shipyard. During March 1922 she sailed from London in atrocious weather under her own power and, after sheltering at Portland, arrived safely at Dumbarton on March 29th. It may have been that *Woolwich Belle* was sold in part-payment of debts owed to the ship-builders.

While *Woolwich Belle* remained idle during the summer of 1921 the other vessels were back in service from the end of July with *Walton Belle* again based in Great Yarmouth. During the season *Walton Belle* made twenty-six trips to Walton and carried 12,557 passengers a figure which, when compared with the numbers reported before the turn of the century, does not seem to be particularly impressive. At the end of September the local agent for the steamers asked the Yarmouth Port Commissioners for a rebate on the dues they had been charged for landing passengers. Whether this claim was successful I've not yet discovered but it does support the view that the number of landings had fallen.

In October 1921 the Shankland brothers, Pickard and De Mattos decided to form yet another company to oversee their steamship operations. This was named the P.S.M. Syndicate after its four directors and was registered on January 1st 1922. Much of the capital used to establish this Company seems to have come from the directors themselves, their families or companies with which they were closely associated. On February 14th 1922, yet another company was registered! It was 'presented for filing' by the P.S.M. Syndicate and was named Belle Steamers Limited. The objectives of this new concern were: "to purchase, hire, take in exchange, charter or otherwise acquire steamships and other vessels or craft of every description and any shares thereof".

The major shareholding in Belle Steamers Limited (9000 shares) was taken by Sackville Investment Trust. This trust seems to have been closely associated with a number of the Shankland brothers' financial enterprises but sadly no records of its activities exist. The remaining large shareholdings went to the P.S.M. Syndicate (6000 shares), The Royal Sovereign Steamship Company (5000 shares), A. W. Pickard (250 shares) and Harold De Mattos (250 shares). The new Company's directors were, not surprisingly, Pickard, De Mattos, the Shankland Brothers and Johannes Brockdorff. Brockdorff was a Norwegian businessman but just why he was appointed a director is unclear. However, it is interesting to note that he was also a director of the General Maritime Trust with which the Shanklands were closely associated! The P.S.M. Syndicate then purchased *Clacton Belle*, *London Belle*, *Southend Belle*, *Walton Belle* and *Yarmouth Belle* from Mr Kingsman for an undisclosed sum. It appears that the *London Belle*, and perhaps other vessels in the fleet were not commissioned that summer, a fact which gives rise to the belief that there was some kind of financial problem during 1922. This surmise is also supported by the fact that I've been unable to find evidence of *Belle* Steamers in Great Yarmouth during the 1922 season. Why this problem occurred is not known, but it almost certainly resulted in Mr Kingsman foreclosing on the steamers' mortgage. In 1923 the five vessels were re-sold to the Royal Sovereign Steamship Company which suggests that it was a purely paper transaction. Indeed the whole 'foreclosure' may have been contrived for some obscure financial reason. Certainly it does not seem to have damaged the directors of the P.S.M. Syndicate in any obvious way and steamer services offered by the Royal Sovereign Steamship Company were well advertised. Two vessels were involved on the Great Yarmouth service, one to, and one from London each day. There was no need for passengers to change at Walton unless they were enjoying a day trip. *Southend Belle* was regularly employed on this service and in late July 1923 showed just how useful the bow rudder could be. Soon after passing Tilbury Fort, she suffered rudder failure but Captain Owen had no hesitation in turning the vessel round and reversing all the way up the Thames to Woolwich, where her passengers were discharged. It appears from this incident that passengers had expected to disembark at Greenwich. This may have been due to mooring problems at Fresh Wharf and indeed, sailings to Great Yarmouth were advertised as leaving from Old Swan Pier. This would have been impossible by a *Belle* Steamer as by this date *Clacton Belle* had long since had her telescopic funnel replaced by one of a fixed design. Small tenders must have ferried passengers to vessels anchored below London Bridge or, perhaps, even to Greenwich.

Although these services were advertised by the Royal Sovereign Steamship Company, it was not the end of the P.S.M. Syndicate, which continued in existence, nor did it mean that the five steamers remained in the ownership of the Royal Steamship Company. It seems probable that, for reasons best known to the directors of the companies involved, the ownership of individual steamers was passed between the companies with which they were concerned.

While these five *Belle* Steamers were engaged in Thames services, the *Woolwich Belle* was not. She had been refitted by Denny's in 1922 and had appeared with a short, rather fat funnel. This may have contributed to her making only 13.29 knots on trials but, for whatever reason, it was lengthened to give a much more pleasing profile. In May 1922 *Woolwich Belle* was sold to The Channel Excursions Limited of Brighton and renamed *Queen of the South*. In 1923 her services along the south

The Medway Queen *was built by Ailsa Shipbuilding and Engineering Company at Troon and went into service during 1924. Apart from war service she remained in the Medway and Thames Estuary until being withdrawn after the 1963 season. In 1966 she became the club-house for a yacht club on the Isle of Wight.*

coast suffered due to the return of three P & A Campbell vessels to the area and in 1924 she was sold to the New Medway Steam Packet Company of Rochester.

The New Medway Steam Packet Company had been formed in December 1919 from the earlier Medway Steam Packet Company. It was an ambitious Company with a dynamic Managing Director, S. J. Shippick. They already owned three old paddle steamers to which they added *Queen of the South*, and planned a fifth, a new vessel to be named *Medway Queen*. Built by the Ailsa Shipbuilding and Engineering Company at Troon, *Medway Queen* was the first paddle steamer to be built for Thames services since the *Golden Eagle* in 1909. She arrived in the Medway in time for the 1924 summer season and was the first of the New Medway Steam Packet Company's self-styled "Queen Line" steamers to be built. However, before she arrived there had been yet another financial upheaval affecting the *Belle* Steamers.

During 1924 the Royal Sovereign Steamship Company had advertised a wide range of services. *Royal Sovereign* was, as usual, employed running to the Kent resorts and in this service she was supported by various *Belle* Steamers. Clacton and Walton were also well provided with services and excursions while the *Belle* Steamer for Great Yarmouth left London Bridge daily, except Friday, at 8.55 a.m. Passengers for this vessel were also able to leave Westminster Pier by a small tender that ferried them to London Bridge. As Fresh Wharf was not available for use during 1924, the *Belle* Steamer timetabled from London Bridge must have been loaded in mid-stream from small boats. Another difference in the service meant that passengers returning to London were required to leave the vessel at either North Woolwich or Greenwich. Those who disembarked at North Woolwich were provided with free rail travel to London Bridge provided they had previously applied to the ship's purser. Being unable to lie overnight at Fresh Wharf required that the vessels should be moored further down stream at Deptford. A similar service was provided in 1925, but even before the season began, financial pressures mounted on the various companies associated with the *Belle* Steamers and *Royal Sovereign*. Indeed, during April, *Walton Belle*, *Yarmouth Belle*, *Southend Belle* and *Clacton Belle* all came up for auction at the Baltic Exchange but, apparently, were soon withdrawn through lack of interest. Only one bid of £16,000 had been made for all four vessels! Quite obviously some form of financial re-structuring became necessary.

For reasons again lost with the records, two new companies were formed in the late Spring of 1925. The first of these was known as the R.S. Steamship Company Limited and it took over some of the Royal Sovereign Steamship Company's assets including *Royal Sovereign* and probably *London Belle*. Unfortunately, the Public Record Office at Kew have no records relating to this new Company but we do know that it traded from the Royal Sovereign Steamship Company's offices at 7 Swan Lane, in the City of London. The remaining assets of the Royal Sovereign Steamship Company together with those of the P.S.M. Syndicate and Belle Steamers Limited, if indeed there were any, were all absorbed into a second company registered on June 18th 1925 as the East Anglian Steamship Company Limited. Its registered offices at 91/93 Bishopsgate were those of the P.S.M. Syndicate and, amongst its directors are found Robert Robertson Shankland and John Hamilton Shankland! I've no reason to doubt that the R.S. Steamship Company had similar names on its Board of Directors. It is also interesting that the nominal capital of the East Anglian Steamship Company was £10,000 divided into

The finishing touches are put to the magnificently decorated paddle box of the Royal Sovereign. *By chance this ornate carving has survived and is now preserved by the Pleasure Steamer Historical Trust.*

An unusual photograph from the 1920s that shows how the funnel of the London Belle *was painted. The light buff colour of the funnel meant this procedure had to be repeated on numerous occasions during the summer season.*

9000 preferential shares at £1 each, and 20000 ordinary shares at 1/- each! This gave rise to a large number of smaller shareholders including retired military men, widows and other married ladies, one of whom was a Gertrude De Mattos!

Neither Belle Steamers Limited not the P.S.M. Syndicate went into receivership, their assets were, it seems, simply transferred. The two former Companies remained in existence as 'hollow shells' and it is probable that the same condition applied to the Royal Sovereign Steamship Company. It appears that this was purely a financial operation that gave an injection of capital to the steamship services. The public would probably have not known that these changes had taken place as the fleet continued to operate much as before and those vessels running to Clacton were still known as the *Belle* Steamers.

In spite of this reconstruction, financial pressures on the *Belle* Steamers continued to mount during 1925 as new competition was experienced both on their Kent and Essex services. During that summer, the New Medway Steam Packet Company opened a new route from the Medway to Felixstowe using *Medway Queen*. The piers once owned by the Coast Development Corporation were now owned by local companies who welcomed any steamship that visited, and especially those as popular as the new *Medway Queen*. The R.S. Steamship Company services to Kent also suffered from improvements to the General Steam Navigation Company's services. In 1925 they took delivery of a new paddle steamer named *Crested Eagle*; the first Thames paddle steamer constructed to burn oil fuel. *Crested Eagle* was certainly a luxurious vessel but, unfortunately, she possessed a squat, ugly appearance, an appearance that was almost certainly attributable to the closure of London's Fresh Wharf. In the previous year, 1924, both *Eagle* and *Golden Eagle* had been forced to move their departure points to Greenwich as they were unable to pass under London Bridge, to the only other available wharf at Old Swan Pier. This gave *Royal Sovereign* a great advantage, as her telescopic funnels enabled her to continue sailing from an established boarding point. *Crested Eagle* was also designed to pass under London Bridge and was equipped with a low superstructure, hinged mast and telescopic funnel. A funnel that was originally divided into three sections! It was these features that gave *Crested Eagle* her unfortunate appearance but, in 1925, enabled her to sail from Old Swan Pier to Margate in direct competition with the old *Royal Sovereign*. Competition was certainly fierce and without doubt contributed to a decision made by the East Anglian Steamship Company during the autumn to sell *Walton Belle*. It was decided to sell this particular vessel because, being very economical, she would command a higher price than any other vessel, except perhaps, *Yarmouth Belle*. In December 1925, *Walton Belle* was purchased by the New Medway Steam Packet Company and taken to their Rochester shipyard where she was renamed *Essex Queen*.

In 1926 *Essex Queen* ran services from Chatham, Sheerness and Southend to Margate while the remaining *Belle* Steamers settled into their old routines. *London Belle* was placed on the long east coast service but had to be withdrawn on July 10th after suffering serious damage while moored at Deptford. In the early hours of the morning she had been run down by the freighter *Kotka* and had sustained severe damage to her stern. *Southend Belle* replaced her and ran to Great Yarmouth as scheduled at 8.45 a.m. By all accounts it was a good season and on the August Bank Holiday Saturday a record number of passengers disembarked at Lowestoft, although, more significant, is that they arrived in one steamer, probably the *London Belle.*

The oil burning Crested Eagle *was launched in 1925. Although not a graceful ship, her three part telescope funnel and hinged mast enabled her to use Old Swan Pier.*

Southwold Belle *approaches Walton Pier on a hazy day in August 1928.* Yarmouth Belle *is already alongside. 1928 was the final year in which* Belle Steamers *operated as a fleet.*

While the services provided by the General Steam Navigation Company and the New Medway Steam Packet Company continued to develop during 1927 and 1928, those of *Belle* Steamers remained static. Indeed, they had even allowed the New Medway Steam Packet Company the opportunity to run *Essex Queen* (ex *Walton Belle*) on the Great Yarmouth to Clacton service! Quite clearly the situation could not continue and it came as no surprise when, soon after the close of the 1928 season, the East Anglian Steamship Company called an extra-ordinary General Meeting of its shareholders. There it was stated that the company "couldn't by reason of its liabilities continue its business and that it was advisable to wind the Company up". Receivers were duly appointed on November 15th 1928 to see to the Company's affairs. Apart from the vessels, the cash assets of the company amounted to £76 3s 0d. Far more than this was owing in wages, salaries and to individuals for "other services rendered". One of the larger debts out standing was £329 12s 7d. owed to the Claremont Pier Company, Lowestoft.

At the same time the R.S. Steamship Company also went into receivership and the assets of both Companies were sold together to pay off their liabilities. At the final winding up meeting of the East Anglian Steamship Company on January 19th 1931, we perhaps find a clue as to just why this period in the history of the *Belle* Steamers has been so difficult to uncover. At the end of the meeting those present passed an "extraordinary resolution" — "that the books, accounts and documents of the company and the liquidators thereof be retained for three months from the date of this meeting and then be destroyed". Fortunately, some documents were overlooked, but I have little reason to doubt that similar resolutions were also passed by the second Royal Sovereign Steamship Company, the R.S. Steamship Company and perhaps, by the other companies with which the *Belle* Steamers had been associated. But this was not quite the end of the story as the companies, *Belle* Steamers Limited and the P.S.M. Syndicate, were still in existence. By 1930 the Companies Registry Office had sent numerous letters enquiring into the financial position of *Belle* Steamers Limited. Eventually, on May 29th 1930, the Registry Office received the following brief communication: "*Belle* Steamers Limited has not been carrying on any business for the past five years. There are no funds in the Company". (Five years previously coincided with the formation of the East Anglian Steamship Company). This response prompted the Companies Registrar to write again seeking further advice. This was not forthcoming and on receiving no replies *Belle* Steamers Limited was finally dissolved on October 7th 1931. The P.S.M. Syndicate had also been the subject of numerous official letters and at the end of March 1931 Robert Shankland wrote to the Joint Stock Companies Registrar stating that the Syndicate had "ceased operations" and "had done no business for some five years". This prompted a reply asking how the Syndicate's assets had been disposed of. Robert Shankland replied that all the Syndicate's assets had been absorbed in paying creditors and that the "capital had been entirely lost". There followed numerous letters from the Companies Registry Office asking if the Syndicate was still trading, but these received no reply. On October 15th, 1932, the P.S.M. Syndicate was "officially dissolved", so ending the story of the companies which had operated the *Belle* Steamer fleet. By this date, the fleet had been dispersed, so it is the continuing story of the ships that provides us with the remainder of this book.

Belle Steamer owner Robert Shankland with his daughter and, what must have been his senior officer, the distinguished Captain Owen. This photograph was taken on the bridge of the Southend Belle *in September 1927.*

During the 1920s Robert Shankland's children established a Walton Belle *on the roof of the garden shed at their home in Limpsfield, Surrey.*

The Royal Sovereign *passes under Tower Bridge during her final year of service as a General Steam Navigation vessel. As her funnels have not been withdrawn, it seems that by this date the bridge was opened to let her pass.*

The diesel powered Queen of the Channel *first appeared in Great Yarmouth during 1937. Her well balanced appearance was created by the fore funnel which was purely cosmetic.* Queen of the Channel *was one of the many vessels that failed to return from Dunkirk in 1940.*

During the early 1930s Laguna Belle (ex-Southwold Belle) *had a distinctive chevron painted on her bow. This can clearly be seen as can the improvements made to Clacton Pier since the Great War.*

The final General Steam Navigation paddle steamer, Royal Eagle was built in 1932 for Thames services. Her rather ugly appearance belied a very comfortable interior which was quite in keeping with the Company's tradition.

Queen of Southend (*ex-*Yarmouth Belle) *approaches Felixstowe Pier during the 1930s. The modifications made to the fore part of the vessel can be clearly seen.*

The Queen of Kent *was built in 1916 originally as the minesweeper* HMS Atherstone. *After being purchased by the New Medway Steam Packet Company in 1928, she was used on cross channel sevices. In 1936 she reopened the long East Coast service to Great Yarmouth.*

EAGLE and QUEEN LINE STEAMERS

1937 SEASON.   **DAILY (Except Fridays).**   (Weather and other circumstances permitting.)

"QUEEN OF SOUTHEND"
(or other Steamer)

From GRAVESEND, Southern Railway Pier (Near the Maidstone District Motor Services Depot)

Leaves Gravesend (West St.)	10.0 a.m.	Leaves Felixstowe	... ...	2.50 p.m.
Arrives Southend	11.0 a.m.	Arrives Walton	... ...	3.30 p.m.
„ Clacton	1.15 p.m.	„ Clacton	... ...	4.15 p.m.
„ Walton	2 p.m.	„ Southend	... ...	6.15 p.m.
„ Felixstowe	2.45 p.m.	„ Gravesend (West St.)	... ...	7.30 p.m. (approx.)

FARES TO SOUTHEND, CLACTON, WALTON & FELIXSTOWE

Single	SOUTHEND 2/- ;	CLACTON 4/- ;	WALTON 4/6 ;	FELIXSTOWE 5/-
Day Return ...	„ 2/- ;	„ 3/9 ;	„ 4/6 ;	„ 5/-
Period	„ 2/6 ;	„ 6/- ;	„ 6/6 ;	„ 7/6

Passengers may also book to Herne Bay and Margate by "Queen of Southend" (changing steamers at Southend). Day Return Fares to Herne Bay 3/9 : to Margate 4/- ; Period Return to Herne Bay 5/6 ; Margate 6/-

ALSO THROUGH BOOKINGS TO

YARMOUTH and LOWESTOFT.
(Change at Clacton)

Fares to YARMOUTH *or* GORLESTON	*Single* 9/6	*Period Return* 14/-
„ „ LOWESTOFT	„ 8/6	„ „ 12/6

Including Gravesend Pier Tolls.   Children under 14 Half Price.   * No luggage allowed to day trip passengers.

CLACTON—LOWESTOFT—YARMOUTH SERVICE.

Leaves Clacton	3.50 p.m.	Leaves Yarmouth	9.40 a.m.
Arrives Lowestoft	7.30 p.m.	„ Gorleston	9.55 a.m.
„ Gorleston	8.15 p.m.	„ Lowestoft	10.45 a.m.
„ Yarmouth	8.30 p.m.	Arrives Clacton	2.50 p.m.

LOCAL AGENTS—Capt. R. W. P. Wilkins, 73, High Street, Gravesend.
Messrs. T. J. Loft & Sons, 39, New Road, and 4, Town Pier, Gravesend.
Book at the Pier.

Bradley & Son, Ltd., 115 Fleet Street, E.C.4 ; and Reading   C 4

After her sale to the New Medway Steam Packet Company, the Walton Belle *was renamed* Essex Queen. *It is possible that the National Deposit Friendly Society had chartered the vessel.*

Old Belles — New Names 7

The *Belle* Steamers may have officially ceased to exist but, to many living along the Suffolk and Norfolk coast all the paddle steamers that came to Great Yarmouth were colloquially referred to as ''*Belles*''. Be they General Steam Navigation or ''Queen Line'' vessels they were, and still are, ''*Belles*''. Probably there is some justification for this misnomer as some of the old *Belles* returned to Great Yarmouth in later years under new ownership and different names. But, for some of the old paddle steamers, the end of the *Belle* steamers was also the end of their working lives.

Worn out and beyond economic reconditioning, two veterans of the fleet, *Clacton Belle* and *London Belle*, were sold to the firm of T. W. Ward and scrapped during 1929. Rather ignominiously they were towed the few miles to their final berths at Grays, Essex, where they were dismantled. *Clacton Belle* had been part of the River Thames life for thirty-eight years and *London Belle* for thirty-five years. The Victorian charm they still possessed was not appreciated in the 'roaring twenties' and soon only memories remained of these fine vessels although, in later years, some items from the *London Belle* have been discovered. Most notable are the ship's wheel and the steam whistle now preserved by the Pleasure Steamer Historical Trust.

Southend Belle and *Yarmouth Belle* were in better condition and consequently did not follow their sisters to the scrapyard. Instead *Yarmouth Belle* was purchased by the New Medway Steam Packet Company (The ''Queen Line''), and renamed *Queen of Southend*. *Southend Belle* was sold to Mr. E. Kingsman, the owner of Clacton Pier, and renamed *Laguna Belle*. Perhaps, like his forebears in 1887, Mr. Kingsman felt a need to secure services to the Pier now that those provided by the East Anglian Steamship Company had ceased. However, although *Laguna Belle* ran a regular summer service to Clacton from June 1930 to August 1935, Mr. Kingsman was never tempted to purchase further vessels.

Royal Sovereign was offered for sale at the same time as the *Belles* and was sold in March 1929 to General Steam Navigation Company for £5,540. This may at first seem rather surprising as *Royal Sovereign* was as old as the *London Belle* and certainly past her prime. However, in the previous August the General Steam Navigation Company had withdrawn the *Eagle* and sold her to Dutch shipbreakers. *Royal Sovereign* was no doubt seen as a popular, if not temporary replacement, prior to the arrival of a new vessel. So, for the summer of 1929 *Royal Sovereign*, once the great rival of The General Steam Navigation Company, ran in their colours to the Thanet resorts.

While *Royal Sovereign* resumed services to her old haunts, the New Medway

Steam Packet Company looked for new routes in the vacuum created by the withdrawal of the *Belle* Steamers, and their attention again fell on Great Yarmouth. Therefore, during 1929, and for the first time in her long career, *Queen of the South* (ex-*Woolwich Belle*) was stationed at Great Yarmouth. From there she ran a daily service to Felixstowe where her arrival coincided with that of *Queen of Southend* (ex-*Yarmouth Belle*). Then, *Queen of the the South* returned to Great Yarmouth via Southwold and Lowestoft while *Queen of Southend* ran back down the coast to Walton, Clacton and Southend before crossing the Thames Estuary to Chatham. Unfortunately, the Great Yarmouth service was not well publicised, and one of the few references in the press to *Queen of the South* occurred after she arrived late on 3rd August 1929, following a particularly rough passage from Felixstowe. During her approach to the Claremont Pier Lowestoft, she had been swept into the piles and forced to abandon her attempt to land passengers. By the close of the season it was evident that the route was uneconomic, and from the final departure of *Queen of the South* in 1929 until the summer of 1936, the route from Great Yarmouth to Felixstowe was abandoned to motor coaches.

The New Medway Steam Packet Company concentrated on the shorter more profitable services. It was the popularity of daily excursions that dictated routes, it was felt that Southwold, Lowestoft and Great Yarmouth were too remote. Felixstowe was about as far north as was practicable for steam excursions based on the Medway ports.

The General Steam Navigation Company also decided to rationalise their services after 1929, and the first victim was the *Royal Sovereign.* ''The grand old lady of the Thames'' was sold for £3,500 to Dutch shipbreakers. Although the new vessel planned by the General Steam Navigation Company had not yet been built, it was probable that, like the *London Belle*, the *Royal Sovereign*'s coal consumption was too heavy to make her services economically viable in a period of economic recession.

Another victim of the cut-backs was Walton-on-the-Naze. It was decided that for 1930 the New Medway Steam Packet Company's vessels should go direct between Clacton and Felixstowe. Walton had not developed as Clacton had and was still regarded as a town in which to spend a 'quiet holiday'. Certainly it attracted a totally different clientele who, generally speaking, stayed for relatively long periods. As in the case of resorts such as Southwold or Aldeburgh, Walton-on-the-Naze was well served by motor coaches which delivered passengers right to their hotels. There was little need to travel by boat and less demand for excursions. Walton had been popular with the *Belle* Steamers because of the facilities its pier possessed rather than because of the trade it attracted.

Conversely, Clacton was a town for the day-tripper! During 1930 *Laguna Belle* (ex-*Southend Belle*) ran from the new Tower Pier to Clacton via Greenwich and Woolwich for four shillings return. A single fare was three shillings and no period returns were issued! She was immensely popular and it has been estimated that she carried an average of nine hundred and thirty passengers each trip. Her owner, Mr. 'Barney' Kingsman, spent £200,000 on improvements to Clacton Pier between 1922 and 1934 and so he probably needed the income generated by *Laguna Belle* to recoup his investment.

At the end of 1930 *Laguna Belle* returned to her builders at Dumbarton for a re-fit which included extending her fore-saloon across the full width of the vessel, in the style of the old *Southwold Belle*. A new boiler was also fitted, but surprisingly she still burned coal. At the same time as *Laguna Belle* was in Scotland *Queen of Southend* (ex-*Yarmouth Belle*) was taken to the New Medway Steam Packet Company's shipyard at Rochester where she joined *Essex Queen* (ex-*Walton Belle*) in a major re-fit which converted them to burn the more economic fuel oil.

The following year, 1931, found both the newly-converted vessels running across the Thames Estuary to Southend, Clacton and Felixstowe or, along the Kent coast to Margate and Ramsgate. A new departure came on Wednesdays when *Essex Queen* was sent up the Thames to Tower Pier so that she could run a cruise around the London Docks, a cruise that was extremely popular with visitors to the City. Another new departure for the New Medway Steam Packet Company was the stationing of their old paddle steamer *City of Rochester* at Ipswich. She ran a daily service to Felixstowe and Clacton where her arrival coincided with that of the Company's vessel from Chatham. It was a service that emulated that of the *Woolwich Belle* some thirty years earlier.

Sadly 1931 was the last year in the long career of *Queen of the South* (ex-*Woolwich Belle*). She was withdrawn by the New Medway Steam Packet Company at the end of the season and laid up pending sale. Unlike the remaining *Belle* Steamers she had not been modernised and so found no buyers. Eventually, after forty-one years of service, she was sent to the scrapyard of Thomas Ward at Grays in July 1932.

While *Queen of the South* was being dismantled, the New Medway Steam Packet Company embarked for the first time on regular services from London. Using either *Essex Queen* or *Queen of Southend* they sailed from Greenwich to Southend, Clacton and Felixstowe. The General Steam Navigation Company retaliated by sending *Crested Eagle* on a new service from London to the Essex resorts. The piers at Clacton and Felixstowe, once closed to General Steam Navigation vessels, were now independently owned and welcomed *Crested Eagle*'s arrival.

The ability of the General Steam Navigation Company to send *Crested Eagle* to Felixstowe was due to the arrival of their long-awaited new paddle steamer *Royal Eagle* in May 1932. Her rather ugly appearance belied a luxurious interior that assured her popularity from the moment she commenced services to Southend, Margate and Ramsgate.

In 1933 the London Docks cruises were run by the General Steam Navigation Company using a newly acquired vessel named *Isle of Arran*. This did not intimidate the New Medway Steam Packet Company who further developed their London services by sending both their old *Belle* Steamers further up the Thames to the traditional steamer berths at Fresh Wharf. From there, both vessels ran daily services to Southend, Herne Bay, Margate and Ramsgate or, to Felixstowe via Greenwich, Woolwich, Southend and Clacton. It was a year in which both *Essex Queen* and *Queen of Southend* were extensively used on the longer excursion trips.

The following year, 1934, was more notable for the construction of one steamer than for any services provided along the Thames. The vessel in question, named *Queen of the Channel*, was built during the winter of 1934/35 as a joint venture by the New Medway Steam Packet Company and William Denny. Denny's were again in the fore front of new design, for *Queen of the Channel* was the first British vessel of her type to be powered by diesel engines, and the first Thames excursion

The City of Rochester *was sent to the River Orwell in 1931 and ran services reminiscent of those provided by* Woolwich Belle. *This photograph, taken early in the century, shows the vessel in the Medway a few yards from where she was destroyed during an air raid in the Second World War.*

Queen of the South *(ex-*Woolwich Belle*) is pictured on the grid at Rochester towards the end of her working life.*

vessel to have been built with propellers since the *Kingfisher* in 1906. Although she suffered from the problems associated with propeller driven steamers, many of these were reduced by improvements in design. As far as her owners were concerned, the main advantage of this vessel was financial. She was much cheaper to operate than conventional paddle steamers of a similar size. Steam engines could not be shut down at pier heads and boilers needed continual feeding by stokers — all this was becoming increasingly expensive. Diesel engines were far less labour-intensive and could be shut down at the flick of a switch. The advantages of such a ship soon became obvious, added to which, *Queen of the Channel* was a very elegant vessel. Her distinctive white hull and super-structure were surmounted by two well-proportioned buff coloured funnels, the forward being a dummy constructed purely to enhance her looks. During the summer of 1935 *Queen of the Channel* became very popular with a new generation of 'trippists' eager for adventure on day excursions to the Continent from Thames and Kent resorts.

While the modern good looks of *Queen of the Channel* caused much aclaim, the ageing *Essex Queen* and *Queen of Southend* quietly moved their London departure point to Tower Pier, so that at times, the three remaining *Belle* Steamers could be seen together in the Pool of London. During September 1935 the General Steam Navigation Company purchased *Laguna Belle* from her Clacton owners. This was the first of two decisive moves made by the General Navigation Company which ultimately led to their dominating the East Coast excursion services.

In 1936 *Laguna Belle* appeared in the colours of her one time rival, The General Steam Navigation Company, on her traditional service to Clacton. She was joined on this service by the *Queen of Southend*, which had undergone major alterations during the previous winter. Her promenade deck had been extended over the full width of the vessel as well as forward to her stem. This completely changed her appearance but not her popularity, and competition with *Laguna Belle* was fierce.

These developments also benefitted Lowestoft as the New Medway Steam Packet Company decided to reopen the Great Yarmouth service. The underlying reasons are rather obscure. Certainly there had been a marked increase in the number of visitors to Great Yarmouth during the long hot summer of 1935 and local excursion boats had done remarkably well. The press agreed that it was the best summer since 1930 and that there seemed ''more money around''. This they suggested marked an upturn in the nation's economic fortunes. Perhaps this had influenced the New Medway Steam Packet Company, or more probably, it was decided to use a surplus vessel to reappraise the route. On June 2nd 1936 the paddle steamer *Queen of Kent* moored at Hall Quay after an inaugural trip. The new daily service (except Friday) ran to Clacton, a repetition of that of the *Belle* Steamers thirty years earlier. *Queen of Kent* was an interesting vessel as she had been built as the Ascot Class paddle minesweeper *H.M.S. Atherstone* and had seen strenuous war service in the English Channel. She and her sister ship *H.M.S. Melton* had been bought by the New Medway Steam Packet Company and had been renamed *Queen of Kent* (1928) and *Queen of Thanet* (1929) respectively. They had been used mostly on services to France but with the acquisition of *Queen of the Channel*, the *Queen of Kent* became available for other coastal excursions. The revival of the Great Yarmouth service was well advertised and by all accounts well patronised. But, although a connection was made at Clacton with *Queen of Southend*, *Crested Eagle* or *Laguna Belle* for a continuation of the journey to London, it was not this through-trade that was sought. By the 1930's the short sea excursions dominated, the longer journeys were the prerogative of the motor coach and the railways. Although often crowded, I suspect that *Queen of Kent* was not being as gainfully employed in Great Yarmouth as she could have been nearer the Thames.

It was in the area of the Thames that profits were made and the General Steam Navigation Company knew it. They also realised that "no passport" trips to the Continent were becoming increasingly popular but, in both areas they were experiencing strong competition from the New Medway Steam Packet Company and their extensive "Queen Line" of steamers. In many ways the "Queen Line" had picked up the services formerly provided by the "*Belle* Line"! But, unlike the early years of the century, the General Steam Navigation Company were not prepared to accept this situation so in early 1937 they made their second decisive move by acquiring a major shareholding in the New Medway Steam Packet Company. It is not within the scope of this book to examine in detail this takeover. Instead, it is enough to say that although the two Companies appeared during the Summer of 1937 as separate concerns, they were in fact one. For the first time in their history the General Steam Navigation Company had a monopoly of steamer services from Southend to Great Yarmouth and they looked to develop it further.

The first indication we have of the General Steam Navigation Company's future plans comes unexpectedly from the Home Secretary, Sir Samuel Hoare's answer to a parliamentary question in June 1937. He stated that weekend trips to the Continent "without passports", would not be possible under the existing laws. He further stated that he was aware of the General Steam Navigation Company's plan to operate Continental services from Great Yarmouth.

Unable to operate weekend trips from Great Yarmouth, the General Steam Navigation Company settled for day trips to Ostende and advertised them widely from July 17th 1937. The motor vessel *Queen of the Channel* left South Quay three times a week at 8 a.m. for Lowestoft's Claremont Pier and for Ostend, where she arrived at 1.45 p.m. After a three hour stay in Belgium she sailed for Great Yarmouth direct, arriving in the Yare at 10.30 p.m. Passengers for Lowestoft were taken there by bus at no extra charge.

As at resorts along the South Coast, these 'no passport' trips were extremely popular with visitors to Great Yarmouth and surrounding towns. However, by all accounts *Queen of the Channel* was a lively seaboat in the shoals off the North Suffolk Coast, and we have a graphic description of sailors with brooms and buckets washing down decks before reaching Lowestoft! Fun though such trips may have been, more significant for our story was the arrival of *Essex Queen* (ex-*Walton Belle*) back in Great Yarmouth. Freshly re-fitted and with a full width fore saloon she replaced *Queen of Kent* for most of the 1937 services to Clacton. Unlike the New Medway Steam Packet Company during the previous year, the General Steam Navigation Company chose not to advertise their coastal services widely, preferring instead to concentrate their advertising on the Ostend excursions. Only occasionally was *Essex Queen* mentioned in the Press and the last sailing was made in mid September, probably by *Queen of Kent*. On this occasion she carried five hundred and thirty passengers for Clacton, one of whom commented favourably on the music played by "radiogram from amidships" — radios had long since replaced orchestras for onboard entertainment. Although I have found one

THE ROYAL SOVEREIGN AT GORLESTON.

During the summer of 1938 the M.V. Royal Sovereign *was a frequent visitor to Great Yarmouth. Her excursions to Ostend cost ten shillings and were very popular. These trips were resumed briefly after the war but not with this* Royal Sovereign *as she was lost in the Bristol Channel during December 1940.*

reference to a Great Yarmouth to Felixstowe service in 1938, this has not been confirmed in spite of extensive searches through contemporary newspapers. I therefore suspect that the five hundred and thirty passengers carried by *Queen of Kent* enjoyed the last service by a paddle steamer to be run down the East Coast from Great Yarmouth. It was the end of an era; a tradition that stretched back to 1866.

During the two remaining summers before World War II, the General Steam Navigation Company concentrated its efforts on Continental excursions and the usual services in and around the Thames Estuary and along the East Coast to Clacton and Felixstowe. With numerous vessels at their disposal, the *Laguna Belle* (ex-*Southend Belle*) and *Essex Queen* (ex-*Walton Belle*) were not confined to one route whereas *Queen of Southend* (ex-*Yarmouth Belle*), renamed *Thames Queen* in 1938, was sent to Tower Pier to run London Dock cruises.

The importance attached by the General Steam Navigation Company to their Continental trips from Great Yarmouth, is reflected in the fact that in 1938 the number of services was increased to four each week and by the appearance of the Company's largest and latest diesel powered vessel, *Royal Sovereign*, in support of *Queen of the Channel*. It was also decided to move the departure point from the congested waters near Haven Bridge to a more suitable, if rather remote berth, at Fish Quay. Perhaps, to the disapointment of those in Lowestoft, the vessels ceased calling at the Claremont Pier and instead, prospective passengers were provided with a connecting bus service to and from Great Yarmouth. However, these excursions did not always go as planned. On August 16th 1938, *Queen of the Channel* sailed for Ostende with over one thousand passengers aboard but she got no further than Gorleston where she struck the South Pier. In my research I have come across numerous incidents of paddle steamers hitting the piers while negotiating the harbour mouth at Great Yarmouth but this was the most serious incident. Caught by the strong tide, *Queen of the Channel* ploughed into the South Pier cutting through a one foot thick wooden pile and making a twenty foot breach in the quay. Passengers were thrown to the deck and many suffered cuts, abrasions and shock. At least eleven required hospital treatment. After twenty minutes Captain T. Aldis extracted *Queen of the Channel* and returned to Fish Quay where passengers had their fares refunded. With her bows severely damaged *Queen of the Channel* returned to London for repairs, and excursions to Ostende were not resumed until August 22nd.

Old Belles Soldier On 8

Soon after the declaration of war on September 3rd 1939, many of the Thames excursion vessels found themselves in the news, when they were employed to transport evacuees from London to 'safer' towns. I have not been able to ascertain whether all the remaining *Belle* Steamers took part in this trek to safety, but certainly *Thames Queen* was involved.

Although the first civilians ever killed by an air raid on British soil had been killed in Great Yarmouth during 1915, that town was considered a ''safety zone'' in 1939. Consequently during early September, seven thousand five hundred children from Dagenham arrived at the 'trawl market'. Over four thousand arrived on one day alone in the General Steam Navigation Vessels, *Queen of the Channel*, *Golden Eagle* and (*Royal*) *Eagle*. I have bracketed 'Royal' as I only suspect that this was the third vessel involved. Newspapers refer to a paddle steamer *Eagle*, but this is clearly a mistake, as to my knowledge, no such vessel with this name existed on the Thames, to my knowledge. It was the first and only time that the famous ''Eagle Steamers'' visited Great Yarmouth, and the first time that two General Steam Navigation paddle steamers had been in the Yare since the Edwardian era.

This evacuation was also the last time that the Claremont Pier, Lowestoft received any vessels alongside. Both *Royal Eagle* and *Royal Daffodil* disembarked children there on the afternoon of September 4th. *Royal Daffodil* was the latest addition to the General Steam Navigation Company's fleet, 1939 being her first season in service. A diesel vessel, *Royal Daffodil* resembled *Queen of the Channel* but was almost twice her tonnage. She had been used exclusively on Continental services from London and was very popular.

Felixstowe Pier was also visited during this exodus from London by *Medway Queen*, *Thames Queen* (ex-*Yarmouth Belle*) and *Crested Eagle*. Again they disembarked children and teachers from City schools.

Soon after this evacuation work had been completed, the General Steam Navigation vessels were requisitioned by the Admiralty. Many of the motor vessels were used to transport the British Expeditionary Force to France, while some of the paddle steamers were fitted out for use as minesweepers. Amongst these were *Laguna Belle* (ex-*Southend Belle*) and *Thames Queen* (ex-*Yarmouth Belle*), both of which were converted during the Autumn. They were fitted with the latest *Oropesa* sweeping equipment which consisted of a large torpedo-shaped 'float' fixed to the end of a cutting wire. This wire was wound round a powerful steam winch that was fitted at the vessel's stern. When sweeping, the float was carefully lowered into the water to be carried away from the vessel by an object that is best described as an underwater kite. Water pressure held the float in position about five hundred yards astern and two hundred and fifty yards off the minesweeper's

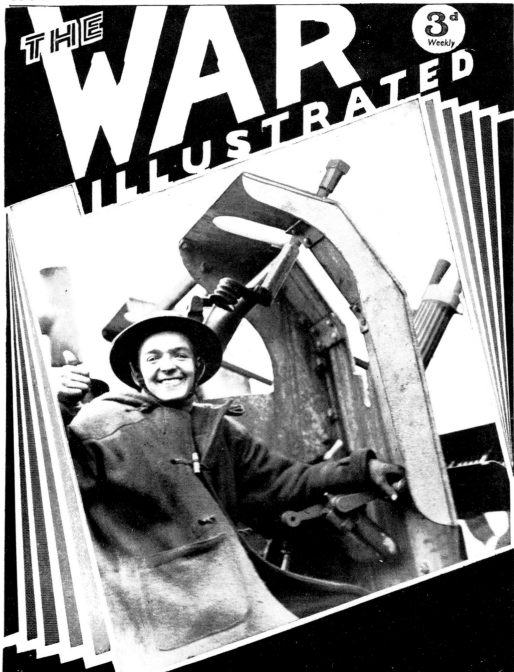

His First Shot from the Old Paddle Steamer Brought Down a Dornier

Although not depicting a Belle Steamer, this front cover of the wartime magazine War Illustrated, *reflects the popular image of paddle steamers at war.*

stern quarter. The 'warp', which stretched back to the winch, then cut mine cables in the conventional manner. Because the paddle steamers had such extensive decks, both the 'old Belles' were fitted with two sets of equipment allowing them to sweep to port and starboard simultaneously.

The extensive decks also made them unpleasantly large targets for enemy aircraft and, although there was room for a considerable number of guns, during the early months of the war these were in short supply. Consequently, when *Laguna Belle* and *Thames Queen* joined the 10th Minesweeping Flotilla they were armed only with a 12 pdr. Anti-Aircraft gun forward and some Lewis guns mounted around the bridge.

The 10th Minesweeping Flotilla was based at Dover and comprised eight paddle steamers of various ages, the two *Belle* Steamers being the oldest. There were two other General Steam Navigation, ''Queen Line'' steamers, in the flotilla, *Medway Queen* and *Queen of Thanet*. The remaining vessels came from various South Coast companies and were the *Sandown, Brighton Belle, Princess Elizabeth* and, the most modern paddle steamer of all, *Gracie Fields*. During that first winter of the war all eight vessels were actively involved in minsweeping in the busy and dangerous waters of ''The Downs''.

The remaining *Belle* Steamer, *Essex Queen*, was also requisitioned as a minesweeper but, whether she was converted is not clear, as early in 1940 she became a hospital ship based on the Thames.

The 10th Minesweeping Flotilla would probably have gone on to become unsung heroes had it not been for the plight of the British Expeditionary Force in May 1940. As the British and French Armies were forced back towards the English Channel by German forces, the Admiralty made plans for their evacuation. On May 14th, the B.B.C. announced that all owners of self-propelled pleasure craft between thirty feet and one hundred feet were to send details to the Admiralty within 14 days. ''Operation Dynamo'' — the evacuation from the beaches of Dunkirk — was soon to commence.

On the evening of May 27th 1940, the eight ships of the 10th Flotilla sailed from Dover in line ahead for the beaches around Dunkirk where, they were informed, ''soldiers would be waiting''. They were, and in the dawn light long lines of men could be seen wading into the water and waiting patiently. Although ordered to leave at dawn, the enormous scale of the operation clearly prevented compliance and, in the sure knowledge of the dangers that daylight would bring, the old paddle steamers began to load soldiers. Thus, small boats, including their own lifeboats, ran a shuttle service to and from the beaches a half mile away. Surprisingly, only a few bombs fell that morning and fortunately they all missed. At about 7 a.m., the Senior Officer (*P.S. Sandown*) ordered the Flotilla away from the beaches and back to Dover. All went well until just off the Kent coast, when a number of enemy aircraft were sighted and engaged by the various ships in the area. Unfortunately, during the frantic manoeuvering that followed, *Brighton Belle* struck the submerged wreck of a ship mined a few hours earlier, and began to sink. *Medway Queen* went alongside and took off eight hundred soldiers, the crew and the Captain's dog before the old paddle steamer sank. The remaining steamers returned to Dover and disembarked their troops. At 2.30 p.m., the store-ship *Dorrien Rose* entered Dover and unloaded nine hundred soldiers and sailors, survivors from the General Steam Navigation Company's motor vessel, *Queen of the Channel*, which had been bombed and sunk on her way back from the beaches.

During the bitter winter of 1939/40, both *Thames Queen* and *Laguna Belle* suffered mechanical problems on a number of occasions and it was probably thought prudent not to send them back into the fray. So, when the 10th Flotilla again assembled late in the afternoon of May 29th, both the old *Belle*s were missing, their Dunkirk adventure over.

This was the last time that the 10th Flotilla sailed as a unit, after this the vessels were dispatched independently, decisions being left to the discretion of the individual Captains. Perhaps the *Belle*s were lucky, because May 29th was a day that saw the destruction of three more paddle steamers. The Scottish paddle steamer *Waverley*, part of the Harwich Flotilla, was the first to go. Bombed, she sank a minute after ''abandon ship'' had been given, taking over three hundred soldiers and many of the ship's company with her. One of the vessels that came to her rescue was the paddle steamer *Golden Eagle*. She had not been fitted out as a minesweeper, but instead, had joined *Crested Eagle* and *Royal Eagle* as ''Thames Special Service Ships''. Designated as Auxiliary Anti-Aircraft Vessels, these three steamers were given a wide range of armaments and were based at Sheerness to aid the defence of Thames shipping. Later that afternoon the paddle steamer *Gracie Fields* was bombed soon after leaving Dunkirk harbour and her engine room was wrecked. After survivors had been transferred the paddle steamer was taken in tow by the minesweeper *Pangbourne*. The tow proved impossible and *Gracie Fields* suffered the ignominy of being sunk by gunfire from the *Pangbourne* not far from the Kent coast. A few hours earlier the *Crested Eagle*, with a complement of soldiers that had been swelled by survivors from an earlier sinking was bombed soon after pulling away from the Dunkirk mole. A bomb landed on the crowded deck between the funnel and the engine room and exploded. Immediately the vessel began to roll over and as it did so the oil fuel ignited so turning the paddle steamer into a blazing inferno that claimed the lives of over three hundred men.

The following month this short poem appeared in *Punch*.

The Day of the Little Ships

Long after the shadow of war is fled
  And the last battle is fought
Men will remember the little ships
  And the great thing they wrought.

We shall tell over with laughter and tears
  The homely names they bore —
They, not meant for the baptism of fire
  And the grim ways of war.

Paddler, dinghy and sailing barge,
  Eagle and *Queen* and *Belle*,
And the humble Martha's of the ports
  That have no name to tell.

Let us remember them and their men
  Who asked not fee nor fame,
But all they knew was a job to do,
  And they spat on their palms and came.

Hiding behind her distinctive camouflage, the Thames Queen *(ex-Yarmouth Belle)rides at anchor in the Thames Estuary. Her 4-barrel Boulton & Paul gun turrets are clearly visible on the bridge wings.*

The numerous anti-aircraft weapons installed on the old paddle steamers after their conversion from minesweepers are seen in this broadside view of Laguna Belle *(ex-Southend Belle).*

They dared the hell of the shell-swept dunes,
  The hell of the bomb-torn tide,
They cared not a damn if they sank or swam
  Nor yet if they lived or died.

Home they came from that coast of death,
  Each with her tale of men,
Stayed but to set them ashore — and so
  Back to hell's mouth again.

Therefore, while England's cliffs shall stand,
  And the Channel Tides do roll,
Let us remember the Little Ships —
How on the Day of the Little Ships
  They saved an army whole.

C.F.S. Punch June 19th 1940

As readers may have realised, the contribution made by the paddle steamers at Dunkirk is a story on its own. However, there is an interesting entry in the log of the *Princess Elizabeth* relevant to our story. It clearly states that at 6.45 a.m., on May 31st, the *Princess Elizabeth* turned over the boats she was using to load soldiers to the *Essex Queen*. There is no official record of any naval or merchant vessel with that name, or similar name, being present at Dunkirk. Certainly it must have been a vessel of considerable size to have required boats for loading and I have little reason to doubt that this ship was the old *Walton Belle*. All types of vessels ventured across the channel during those hours of need and a ship the size of the *Essex Queen* would have been of great value, especially if she had been fitted as a hospital ship. Exact records of vessels at Dunkirk are incomplete and a number of vessels officially absent have since been proved as having been present. *Essex Queen* was seen in Dover shortly before "Operation Dynamo" and I feel quite sure her Captain would have taken advantage of the freedom granted to individual skippers and acted on his own initiative and sailed to Dunkirk.

Once 'Dunkirk' was over, *Laguna Belle* and *Thames Queen* returned to minesweeping duties and records relating to them become rather vague. The next definite information is of their forming part of the 8th Minesweeping Flotilla based at South Shields. Here, along with six other paddle steamers they were actively engaged in work along the North East coast where a large German minefield had been discovered. Attacks by enemy aircraft had increased and both vessels had been given extra defensive armament. The most interesting piece of equipment was the 'Holman Projector', described by the *Thames Queen*'s Gunnery Officer as the most frightening thing he ever handled during the war. It consisted of a steel barrel into which was placed a Mills bomb (hand grenade!). This was fired into the air by steam or compressed air where it exploded. It was hoped that the explosion would deter, if not destroy, low flying aircraft. In truth, it probably did more damage to the vessel firing it than to attacking aircraft as the propellant was not always sufficient to project the bomb very far from the ship. The explosion often scattered shrapnel about the deck and shook equipment lose. On one occasion after a night attack on *Thames Queen*, a Mills bomb was discovered jammed in the projector's barrel. Fortunately it was safely removed and "consigned to the deep" before it did any damage! Far more effective for protection were the numerous machine guns that the paddle steamers had 'acquired' from grateful soldiers on their return from Dunkirk.

As the threat of aerial attack continued to grow in late 1941, we have a report of *Thames Queen* and other vessels in the flotilla being equipped with barrage balloons for their defence. These balloons certainly acted as a deterrent as their fixing wires would rip the wing off any aircraft unfortunate enough to hit one but, sadly, the large cumbersome balloons made wonderful targets for an aircraft's machine guns! Also carried during the period at South Shields was a number of depth charges. These were not intended for use against submarines but rather as a means of destroying the new magnetic mines being dropped by German aircraft. These mines could not be swept in the conventional way as they were not attached to wires and did not require to have any actual contact with a vessel before exploding. They lay on the sea bed and were detonated by the magnetic field of a ship passing close to it. Depth charges were dropped in areas where magnetic mines were supposed to be, in the hope that they would destroy them. This seldom happened and these mines remained a problem until more sophisticated means of 'neutralising' were devised.

While *Laguna Belle* and *Thames Queen* were busy minesweeping in the North East, *Essex Queen* (ex-*Walton Belle*) was almost certainly operating in the Thames Estuary. At one time she was under the command of Commodore Branthwaite, who was a popular Thames paddle steamer captain during the 1930s. Attached to the Port of London Authority, *Essex Queen* was used to aid relief work after the heavy German bombing raids on London's dockland. It was in this hospital ship capacity that she continued to serve until 1943 when with "The Blitz" over, conditions permitted her withdrawal. Unlike the other two *Belle* Steamers, *Essex Queen* was returned from Admiralty service in March 1943 and spent the rest of the war in obscurity.

This was not to be the fate of either *Laguna Belle* or *Thames Queen*. From 1940 there had been a steady growth in the number of purpose-built minesweepers in naval service and during 1942 it was decided to withdraw the majority of paddle minesweepers for conversion into auxiliary anti-aircraft ships for coastal defence. This was especially needed in the Thames Estuary where air attacks on coastal convoys waiting to move up-river were being particularly effective. *Laguna Belle* and *Thames Queen* were both refitted and had most of their minesweeping equipment removed. This was replaced by an increased armament that included four 20 mm guns and two Boulton and Paul aircraft gun turrets, housing eight .303-machine guns. In addition there were two 2 lb anti-aircraft guns and a number of light machine guns. In spite of being heavily armed, the paddle steamers lacked any sophisticated gunnery control and although they did shoot down a number of enemy aircraft, it was in breaking up attacking formations that they were particularly effective. Both *Laguna Belle* and *Thames Queen* were seen in this rôle at Sheerness and Harwich on numerous occasions during 1942 and 1943.

Although *Thames Queen* continued in the capacity of an anti-aircraft vessel until the end of hostilities, *Laguna Belle* did not. By the beginning of 1944 *Laguna Belle* was beginning to show her age and in January 1944 was sent to the South Coast as an accommodation vessel, her active war career over. With the preparations for the Normandy landings increasing, there was a growing need for all sorts of accommodation vessels around our shores and *Laguna Belle* was just one of a number of paddle steamers that were relegated to this important, if glamourless, rôle. *Laguna Belle* remained in this capacity until released from Admiralty service in July 1946. *Thames Queen*, now elaborately camouflaged, was also sent to the South Coast, probably in 1944, and there she remained actively engaged until the war ended. She was then laid up, although perhaps as an accommodation vessel, until being released by the Admiralty in March 1947.

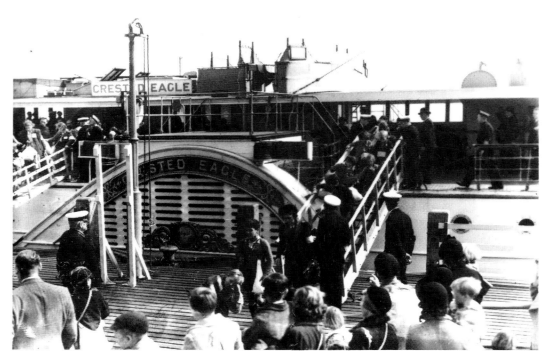

A poignant moment for many evacuated children as they disembark from the Crested Eagle *at Felixstowe Pier in September 1939. It was probably the last time that the vessel berthed at Felixstowe as* Crested Eagle *was sunk in 1940.*

The Final Chapter **9**

As had been the case in the Great War, all the remaining *Belle* Steamers survived the conflict that had cost the General Steam Navigation Company four of their excursion fleet: *Crested Eagle, City of Rochester, Queen of the Channel* and *Royal Sovereign.* However, duties under the White Ensign had taken its toll of the old vessels and with the austerity of post war years the future looked bleak. *Laguna Belle* (ex-*Southend Belle*) ended her naval duties on the South Coast, probably at Southampton as she was moored near the Royal Pier awaiting the decision of her owners as to her future. It wasn't long in coming and as expected *Laguna Belle* was condemned and towed away to Dutch shipbreakers on October 13th 1946. *Thames Queen* (ex-*Yarmouth Belle*) remained under Admiralty orders for longer but on being released was found to be unfit for reconditioning and was laid up, still camouflaged at Southampton. In 1948 she was sold to Metal Industries Ltd and demolished at Dover.

The last *Belle* Steamer, *Essex Queen* (ex-*Walton Belle*) was more fortunate than her sisters as she had been returned to her owners in March 1943 and consequently was in better condition. She was sold to the South Western Steam Navigation Company of Totnes in December 1945, for reconditioning and further use in Torbay. This new company had been formed by three local businessmen of whom two were closely associated with the boatbuilders, Alan Curtis Ltd., whose Head Office was in Totnes. In mid-July 1947, refitted, but still retaining her bridge behind her funnel, the old *Walton Belle*, now renamed *Pride of Devon* appeared at the Haldon Pier Torquay, offering "three glorious cruises daily". These cruises were a morning trip to Dawlish (five shillings) and a three hour afternoon trip to Start Bay (seven shillings and sixpence). In the evening a "moonlight cruise", reminiscent of those once offered by *Woolwich Belle* on the Orwell, was given around Torbay (three shillings and sixpence).

There were other cruises along the coast, most notable being one in late August when *Pride of Devon* gave three hundred children from local orphanages a cruise to Teignmouth and Dawlish. Much to the exitement of the children, this trip culminated in the rescue of two people found clinging to an upturned boat.

In an effort to increase bookings, the South Western Steam Navigation Company advertised cruises accompanied by displays of "adagio and acrobatic dancing" or entertainments by the "Torbay Follies". There was even a "sensational trapeze act" that gave a display from the masthead! How removed this was from the lifestyle that had led to the building of *Walton Belle*! The elegance that still adorned the saloons seemed somewhat out of place. I have often wondered what Penfold and those other eminent Victorians who, fifty years earlier had sailed down Loch Long, would have thought!

TORBAY, THE EVENING TRIP.

In the twilight of her career the Pride of Devon *(ex-*Walton Belle*) steams across Tor Bay on an evening cruise. Her Devon services ceased in 1948, after which the vessel was laid up.*

Unfortunately, it seems that if the *Pride of Devon* was to survive, such bizaare entertainments were required. The old vessel was past her prime and was expensive to maintain in comparison with the growing number of smaller pleasure boats that were appearing around our coasts. In particular, the ex-Admiralty Fairmile motor launches were proving very popular. These diesel powered launches, surplus to requirements were being sold at very reasonable prices and were ideal for conversion to excursion vessels. Also, *Pride of Devon* suffered from an inability to land passengers at beaches. Beach landings, were particularly popular along the South West coast but required modifications that were probably not possible on a vessel the size of *Pride of Devon*.

In 1948 *Pride of Devon* returned to Torquay and resumed services similar to those of the previous year. However, on July 13th she was involved in a tragic accident that was to mar her final year of service. Soon after leaving Paignton on the short journey to Brixham, *Pride of Devon* was approached by the small motor launch *Devonshire Maid*. On the paddle steamers bridge, Captain A. Aldis watched the launch but, as he had the right of way, he was not unduly concerned until it became obvious that *Devonshire Maid* was keeping to her course. Before Captain Aldis could take evasive action, the launch passed under the steamers bow with disastrous consequences. The stem of the paddle steamer sliced through the flimsy wooden sides of the motor launch cutting it in two. Passengers on *Devonshire Maid* who had not already followed their skippers command to "jump for it" were thrown into the water and clung to whatever wreckage they could find. While nearby boats hurried to the scene, some of the crew from the *Pride of Devon* jumped overboard in an attempt to rescue those within reach. Survivors were taken to Brixham where a fleet of ambulances ferried them to hospital but, sadly, two elderly ladies on holiday in the area were drowned. At the subsequent enquiry, Captain Aldis was exonerated when it was stated that "no blame could be attached to the *Pride of Devon*". The *Devonshire Maid* had clearly not observed the "rules of the road" and it was suggested very forcefully that more care should be taken when issuing licences to pleasure boat operators.

Undamaged, *Pride of Devon*'s services continued and in late July she was given permission to land at Dartmouth. It seems fitting that some of the paddle steamer's last excursions were to this picturesque, rather old fashioned town. In the Spring of 1949, *Pride of Devon* was surveyed for her passenger certificate but owing to "defects" this was refused. Beyond economic repair, the old steamer was again laid up at Southampton, where, gradually deteriorating, she was to linger for a further two years. In March 1951, she was sold to the shipbreakers, T. W. Ward, and made her final voyage under tow to their wharf at Grays Essex, where she was dismantled. On reflection, perhaps the Thames was the most fitting place for the old *Walton Belle* to end her days, for it was along that river that she had sailed for so many years. The Thames still flows quietly to the sea but, only memories remind us of *Walton Belle* and that fleet of steamers that once brought visitors in their thousands to the resorts of Kent and the east coast: the fleet that will always be affectionately remembered as the "*Belle* Steamers".

Under the watchful eye of Captain Smith some of the last passengers to board a vessel of the Belle *fleet step aboard* Yarmouth Belle *at Felixstowe in September 1928.*

Postscript

The 1950's marked not only the end of the last "*Belle* Steamer" but it also heralded a rapid decline in the fortunes of paddle steamers generally. The General Steam Navigation Company scrapped *Golden Eagle* and *Royal Eagle* in 1951 and 1953 respectively. However, they continued their Thames operations with diesel vessels until 1966. This famous company was later absorbed by European Ferries, now part of the P. & O. Group. In 1963 a company was registered as New Belle Steamers in order to experiment with small scale paddle steamer operations on the Thames. Services lasted only a few days before its one vessel, the Victorian paddle steamer *Consul*, was returned to its South Coast owners. The experience gained probably helped the Paddle Steamer Preservation Society to preserve their *Waverley*, which today, is the world's last sea-going paddle steamer.

Other paddle steamers may be found in various static roles around our coasts but the only one which has had a small part in our story is the *Medway Queen*. In 1984 this historic vessel was rescued in a dilapidated condition from the Isle of Wight and is now the subject of a long-term restoration project on the Medway. Perhaps one day she will again sail the waters of the Thames Estuary, bringing joy to thousands.

Afloat, but only with the aid of pumps, the Medway Queen *is towed down the River Medway during November 1987.* Medway Queen *is the sole surviving example of a Thames Coast paddle steamer.*

Appendix

Belle Differences 1889-1930

When looking at vessels in the *Belle* fleet one is almost always confused by the similarities in design. Indeed, the individual ships are notoriously difficult to differentiate, one from the other, although, as a fleet they were readily identifiable. The reason for this problem is simple; they were, with the exception of the *Clacton*, designed and built along similar lines by Denny Brothers of Dumbarton. This has since been referred to as the "copyright" Denny pattern. It has taken me many years to become moderately competent in identifying individual *Belle* Steamers and even now, I sometimes have to admit failure. I hope that this section may help readers to identify photographs or postcards they may have.

All the *Belle* Steamers had one pole mast made of pitch pine that was placed forward of the upper promenade deck. Only on *Clacton Belle*, *Woolwich Belle* and *London Belle* was this originally hinged and I have not seen a photograph of any mast lowered. Each had a single, buff-coloured funnel on top of a white superstructure and black hull. *Woolwich Belle* and *Clacton Belle* were the only two members of the fleet to be built with telescopic funnels, enabling them to use the Old Swan Pier but most photographs show these vessels after their funnels had been replaced by one of a "fixed" design. As with all Thames paddle steamers of this era, the captain's bridge stretched between the paddle boxes and was placed aft of the funnel to comply with Thames by-laws. It was felt that such a position eased navigation when going astern, a feature which was common on the Thames between Greenwich and London Bridge, and on the Yare, where either the journey up or down was made going astern. However, it did not aid navigation when out at sea and may have contributed to a number of accidents. In the *Belle* Steamers the forward saloon, with the promenade deck on top, did not extend forward of the mast and therefore, left an open well deck at the bow. Both *Clacton Belle* and *Woolwich Belle* were originally built with the saloon stopping well short of the mast but, in both cases, it was later altered to resemble those of the other vessels in the fleet. Denny's fitted each vessel with two eighteen feet yellow pine, clinker built lifeboats fitted aft of the paddle box, one to port and one to starboard. After 1912 two extra lifeboats were fitted to the quarterdeck of all the vessels in the fleet with the exception of *Woolwich Belle*. With all these similarities it is not surprising that identification is confusing. However, there were differences and I hope to reveal some of these by examining individual vessels.

Clacton Belle

Early photographs of this ship show her with a black telescopic funnel and a short upper promenade deck that stopped well short of the mast. The promenade deck was lengthened and a fore saloon fitted at about the time *Belle* Steamers started to use Fresh Wharf in 1893. At the same time the funnel was replaced by one of a conventional design. Although this funnel resembled that of the *London Belle* it was noticeably taller and is a distinctive feature in photographs. Again, like *London Belle*, the funnel sits on a round base and has the steam whistle placed on the front and the exhaust pipes at the rear. When seen alongside other *Belle*s the mast is also seen to be much shorter and was hinged. Another distinctive feature was the aft saloon as this was much longer than her sisters' and, if one counts them, has many more windows. The wheel for the bow rudder was placed in the well deck forward. Although *Clacton Belle* was a popular vessel and much photographed, I have seen few postcards depicting her.

Woolwich Belle

Said to be the most easily identifiable of the steamers as she was significantly shorter than the other vessels of the fleet. Certainly, in her early years of service on the Orwell, she is easily recognised by her telescopic funnel and large set of steps leading from the promenade deck to the well deck. Soon after the turn of the century the funnel was replaced by one of a ''fixed'' design and a bow rudder added, the wheel for which was sited in the well deck. As she was based for so long at Ipswich, it is not surprising that there are many postcards showing her on the Orwell and in the immediate vicinity. After her withdrawal from Ipswich, the saloon was extended forward to the mast and across the full width of the ship. Following this modification she looks more like the *Southwold Belle* than any other member of the fleet.

London Belle

This seems to be the most commonly photographed *Belle* Steamer and was probably the most prestigious command. A number of postcards exist showing her on the Thames and especially near Fresh Wharf. Being the largest member of the fleet made her very distinctive, added to which she was given a very tall funnel fixed to a round base. This could easily lead to confusion with the *Clacton Belle* but, if one compares the number of rectangular saloon windows, *London Belle* has noticeably fewer. As with the first four members of the fleet, the steam whistle was fixed to the front of the funnel while the exhaust pipes were placed at the rear. The wheel for the bow rudder was placed at the forward end of the promenade deck but was set a little further aft than those on later vessels. Although the mast was hinged on a tabernacle and rested on a crutch, these features are not easily seen in photographs.

Southend Belle

Another prestigious command, the *Southend Belle* was given a much shorter, broader funnel than that of *London Belle*; a funnel closely resembling those of the final three *Belle* Steamers. However, unlike the later ships this was mounted on a round base and had the whistle in front and the exhaust pipes behind. *Southend Belle* was unique in having a very large ventilator situated just behind the bridge and this conspicuous feature can often be seen in photographs. *Southend Belle* carried the wheel for the bow rudder at the forward end of the promenade deck which, on reflection seems a much more sensible position as communication with the bridge would be easier. *Southend Belle* was a popular subject for photographers and there are a large number of postcards showing her at Great Yarmouth.

Walton Belle

This vessel is more often confused with her almost identical sister, *Yarmouth Belle*, than with any other member of the fleet. Although she was ten feet shorter than *Yarmouth Belle* this difference cannot be seen in photographs and is of no practical use. *Walton Belle* was given a short, broad funnel, rather like that of *Southend Belle*, except that it was fixed to a square base. Unlike any of the earlier vessels, both the steam whistles and exhausts were placed at the front of the funnel in a pattern to be followed by both the later steamers. Like the *Southend Belle*, the wheel for the bow rudder was placed at the forward end of the promenade deck and many photographs show this feature. Because of her smaller size, *Walton Belle* carried fewer ventilators than the earlier vessels but I have yet to find a photograph in which I can count them! As *Walton Belle* was a popular visitor to Great Yarmouth, there are many postcards showing her in the Yare although, I fear, some purporting to depict *Walton Belle* may show *Yarmouth Belle*.

Yarmouth Belle

Apart from being slightly larger, *Yarmouth Belle* was almost identical with *Walton Belle* and differences cannot be seen in photographs. It has been said that *Yarmouth Belle* carried the wheel for the bow rudder in the well deck, rather like that of the *Clacton Belle* but, I can find no evidence to support this theory. Indeed, photographs that have been positively identified as *Yarmouth Belle* clearly show the wheel at the forward end of the promenade deck, a position that is supported by the original Denny plans.

Southwold Belle

Southwold Belle is probably the most readily identifiable *Belle* Steamer for, although she was built as a virtual repeat of the *Yarmouth Belle*, she was significantly different. For an undisclosed reason, Denny's placed the wheel for the bow rudder in the well deck and this feature can often be seen in photographs of the vessel approaching a pier. Another difference was that the fore saloon extended across the full width of the vessel and was provided with windows that were identical with those of the aft saloon. Only later was the smaller *Woolwich Belle* to have this feature. Also, when seen alongside *Walton Belle*, the distance between the funnel and the mast is noticeably longer and indeed, the promenade deck almost touches the mast. *Southwold Belle* was sold in 1912 and, at sometime between then and the outbreak of the Great War, she had her bridge moved forward of the funnel and the promenade deck extended back, almost to her stern. Although this vessel was in service for a shorter time than any other *Belle* Steamer, her services are well recorded pictorially and postcards depicting her are frequently found.

The only other vessel belonging to the fleet was the *Clacton* built in 1888. The only photographs I have seen of her show the vessel in Turkish waters and, as she was in London only for one season, I doubt that many views of her on the Thames have survived.

The following tables relate only to vessels mentioned within this book and have been arranged by company ownership. Where ownership of a vessel changed within the scope of this book, the vessel is listed under its original owner's name.

The Belle Steamers

NAME	DATE BUILT	WHO/ WHERE	DIMENSIONS	MACHINERY TYPE	N.H.P.**	GROSS TONS	FATE
Clacton Belle	1890	Denny Brothers Dumbarton	246′ × 35½′ × 14′ + 5¼′	Compound diagonal 28″/50″ × 60″	183	458	Scrapped Grays 1929
Woolwich Belle	1891	Denny Brothers Dumbarton	200′ × 24′ × 8′ + 5′4″	Compound diagonal 24″/42″ × 54″	117	298	Scrapped Grays 1932
London Belle	1893	Denny Brothers Dumbarton	249′ × 30′ × 11½′ + 7′4¼″	Diagonal triple expansion* 29½″/44″/64″ × 72″	364	738	Scrapped Grays 1929
Southend Belle	1896	Denny Brothers Dumbarton	249′ × 30′ × 10½′ + 6½′	Diagonal triple expansion 28″/41½″/60″ × 60″	203	570	Scrapped Holland 1946
Walton Belle	1897	Denny Brothers Dumbarton	230′ × 26′ × 9¾′ + 6′4″	Diagonal triple expansion 20½″/30″/43″ × 60″	105	465	Scrapped Grays 1951
Yarmouth Belle	1898	Denny Brothers Dumbarton	240′ × 28′ × 9¾′ + 6′4¾″	Diagonal triple expansion 20½″/30″/43″ × 60″	105	522	Scrapped Dover 1948
Southwold Belle	1900	Denny Brothers Dumbarton	245′ × 28′ × 9¾′ + 6′4″	Diagonal triple expansion 20½″/30″/43″ × 60″	105	535	Scrapped Genoa 1925

*The first three crank paddle engine built by Denny

**N.H.P. = Nominal Horse Power

The dimensions are recorded as length (overall) × breadth × depth (from main deck) + draught (at full load)

Machinery type = Cylinder diameter × length of stroke.

The London, Woolwich and Clacton-on-Sea Steamship Company.

P.S. Clacton

NAME	DATE BUILT	WHO/ WHERE	DIMENSIONS	MACHINERY TYPE	N.H.P.**	GROSS TONS	FATE
Clacton	1888	J. Scott & Co. Kinghorn	189′5″ × 22′2″ × 8′3″	Compound diagonal 28″/57″ × 57″	204	241	To Turkey as *Aidin* Scrapped 1913(?)

Early Thames paddle steamers owned by the London Steamboat Company and its successors.

NAME	DATE BUILT	WHERE	DIMENSIONS	TONS	FATE
Queen of the Orwell	1862	Govan	171'6" × 18'5" × 7'9"	165	Fairy Queen 1891 scrapped
Queen of the Thames	1861	Woolwich	158' × 19' × 8'2"	143	Scrapped 1889
Duke of Connaught (ex *Ardencaple*)	1866	Port Glasgow	159'1" × 16'1" × 6'4"	127	Scrapped 1889
Duke of Cambridge (ex *Ardgowan*)	1866	Port Glasgow	150'8" × 16'1" × 6'2"	92	Scrapped 1898 (?)
Duke of Teck (ex *Leven*)	1866	Port Glasgow	150'2" × 16'2" × 6'2"	93	Scrapped 1889 (?)
Duke of Edinburgh (ex *Craigrownie*)	1865	Port Glasgow	175' × 17'1" × 6'8"	123	Scrapped 1898 (?)
Alexandra*	1865	Port Glasgow	230'5" × 22'2" × 8'5"	279	Wrecked 9/1889 and scrapped
Princess Alice (ex *Bute*)	1865	Greenock	219'4" × 22'2" × 8'4"	252	Lost 9/1878
Albert Edward (ex *Kyles*)	1865	Greenock	219'4" × 22'2" × 8'4"	252	Scrapped 1888

Alexandra had been intended for use as a blockade runner during the American Civil War but the conflict had ended before her completion.

NAME	DATE BUILT	WHERE	DIMENSIONS	TONS	FATE
Sibyl	1844	Blackwall	114'5" × 13'5" × 6'9"	82	wrecked 3/1863
Bride	1839	London	93'5" × 13'6" × 6'9"	121	wrecked 8/1859
Vale of Clwyd	1865	Rutherglen	186'5" × 18'7" × 7'	173	(?)
Glen Rosa	1877	Greenock	206'1" × 20'1" × 5'	254	Scrapped Bristol 1921

Vessels managed by the Victoria Steamboat Association.

NAME	DATE BUILT	WHERE	DIMENSIONS	GROSS TONS	FATE
Lord of the Isles	1877			451	Renamed Jupiter Scrapped
Victoria	1886	Port Glasgow	222'4" × 23'1" × 8'	341	Destroyed by fire Glasgow 1897
Koh-i-Noor	1892	Govan	300'4" × 32'1" × 10'6"	884	Scrapped Morecambe 1918
Royal Sovereign	1893	Govan	300'2" × 33'1" × 10'6"	891	Scrapped Holland 1930
La Marguerite	1894	Govan	350' × 40' × 13'6"	1,554	Scrapped 1925
La Belgique	1875	Govan	220' × 25' 2" × 11'	484	Wrecked 1905

The General Steam Navigation Company

The vessels outlined below are only those mentioned in the text. The extensive G.S.N.C. coastal fleet contained many other paddle or screw steamships.

NAME	DATE BUILT	WHERE	DIMENSIONS	TONS	FATE
Hoboken	1873	Glasgow	222'4" × 22'9" × 10'5"	413	Scrapped 1898
Sir Walter Raleigh *	1858	Renfrew	168'5" × 20'6" × 10'4"	239	Sold/Scrapped (?) 1891
Eagle	1898	Dundee	265' × 30'1" × 10'1"	647	Scrapped Holland 1928

*There is some disagreement over the dates attributed to Sir Walter Raleigh

The General Steam Company's "Classical Birds"

NAME	DATE BUILT	WHERE	DIMENSIONS	GROSS TONS	FATE
Halcyon	1887	Kinghorn*	209'2" × 26'2" × 9'1"	458	Scrapped (?)
Mavis	1888	Kinghorn	210'3" × 26'3" × 9'4"	474	Scrapped 1915
Oriole	1888	Kinghorn	230' × 27'6" × 9'8"	484	Sold 1912 Hulked
Laverock	1889	Kinghorn	210'2" × 26'2" × 9'4"	470	Scrapped 1922
Philomel	1889	Kinghorn	236' × 27'1" × 9'5"	564	Scrapped 1913

*All vessels built by J. Scott & Company

The General Steam Navigation Company's *"Continental Steamers"*

NAME	DATE BUILT	WHERE	DIMENSIONS	GROSS TONS	FATE
Swallow	1875	Stockton-on-Tees	200'5" × 27'2" × 14'5"		Scrapped 1901
Swift	1875	Stockton-on-Tees	200'5" × 27'2" × 14'5"		Sold and scrapped 1902
Moselle	1852	West Ham	198'5" × 25'5" × 14'6"	516	Scrapped
Rhine	1849	London	190'2" × 25'8" × ?	441	Scrapped
Seine	1849	West Ham	175' × 23'3" × 13'1"	336	Scrapped 1891

General Steam Navigation Company vessels built or acquired after 1900.

NAME	DATE BUILT	WHERE	DIMENSIONS	GROSS TONS	FATE
Kingfisher*	1906	Dumbarton	275' × 32'1" × 10'2"	982	Sold 1912 Scrapped Hong Kong 19??
Golden Eagle	1909	Clydebank	275'7" × 32'1" × 10'1"	793	Scrapped 1951
Crested Eagle	1925	Cowes	299'7" × 34'6" × 11'1"	1,110	Bombed and sunk Dunkirk 29-5-1940
Royal Eagle	1932	Birkenhead	289'9" × 36'5" × 11'5"	1,538	Scrapped 1953
Isle of Arran	1892	Rutherglen	210' × 24'1" × 7'4"	313	Scrapped 1936

*Turbine steamer.

Vessels of the New Medway Steam Packet Company (mentioned in text).

NAME	DATE BUILT	WHERE	DIMENSIONS	GROSS TONS	FATE
City of Rochester	1904	Kinghorn	160'2" × 22'2" × 7'3"	235	Bombed 1941 and scrapped
Medway Queen	1924	Troon	179'9" × 24'2" × 7'6"	316	Undergoing long-term restoration. Medway.
Queen of Kent (ex H.M.S. Atherstone)	1916	Troon	235'2" × 29'1" × 9'2"	798	1948 Sold. Renamed 'Lorna Doone' scrapped 1952
Queen of Thanet (ex H.M.S. Melton)	1916	Port Glasgow	234'9" × 29'1" × 9'2"	792	1948 Sold Renamed Solent Queen Scrapped 1951

General Steam Navigation/New Medway Steam Packet Company
Motor Vessels

NAME	DATE BUILT	WHERE	DIMENSIONS	GROSS TONS	FATE
Queen of the Channel	1935	Dumbarton	255′ × 34′ × 11′6″	1,030	Bombed and sunk off Dunkirk 28-5-1940
Royal Sovereign	1937	Dumbarton	269′6″ × 47′ × 9′1″	1,527	Mined and sunk in the Bristol Channel 9-12-1940
Royal Daffodil	1939	Dumbarton	299′7″ × 50′1″ × ?	2,060	Scrapped Ghent 1967

N.B. All three vessels built by Denny Brothers.

Miscellaneous Thames steamers.

NAME	DATE BUILT	WHERE	DIMENSIONS	GROSS TONS	FATE
Bonnie Doon	1876	Rutherglen	218′ × 20′ × 7′·5″	272	Scrapped 1913
Consul	1896	London	175′ × 20′6″ × 8′2″	257	Scrapped 196?

Select Bibliography

ADAMSON, S. H. *Seaside Piers,* Batsford 1977

BURTT, F. *Cross Channel and Coastal Paddle Steamers,* Tilling 1935

BURTT, F. *Steamers of the Thames and Medway,* Tilling 1949

COX, B. *Paddle Steamers,* Blandford Press 1979

COX, B. *Pleasure Steamers,* David & Charles 1983

DIVINE, A. *Dunkirk,* Faber 1945

DIX, F. L. *Royal River Highway,* David & Charles 1985

HAMBLETON, F. C. *Famous Paddle Steamers,* Percival Marshall 1948

JACOBS, N. *The Sunshine Coast,* Tyndale + Panda Publishing 1986

THE NATIONAL MARITIME MUSEUM, *The Denny Lists,* 1973

THORNTON, E. C. B. *Thames Coast Pleasure Steamers,* T. Stephenson & Sons 1972

THORNTON, E. C. B. *South Coast Pleasure Steamers,* Stevensons 1969

Index

150